HANDBOOK

OF THE

BELGIAN ARMY.

PREPARED BY THE

GENERAL STAFF, WAR OFFICE

1914.

The Naval & Military Press Ltd

Published by

The Naval & Military Press Ltd
Unit 10 Ridgewood Industrial Park,
Uckfield, East Sussex,
TN22 5QE England

Tel: +44 (0) 1825 749494
Fax: +44 (0) 1825 765701

www.naval-military-press.com
www.military-genealogy.com

CONTENTS.

APPENDICES.

THE BELGIAN ARMY.

CHAPTER I.

CONDITIONS OF SERVICE AND NUMBERS AVAILABLE IN WAR.

THE Belgian Army is nominally recruited on the principle of voluntary enlistment supplemented by conscription. The annual contingent is fixed at 13,300 men, and the number of volunteers in any commune is deducted from the quota to be furnished by it.

Every Belgian during his twentieth year must register his name for participation in the drawing of lots. There are exemptions for family and medical reasons, and certain classes and professions are excused service in peace time, but on mobilization for war they are liable to be called out and employed in civil capacities with the army.

The quota of conscripts, who are known as "*miliciens*," to be furnished in each commune is made up from those registered who draw the lowest numbers. Substitutes are allowed, all arrangements being made by the military authorities. Applications are dealt with in the order of priority established in the drawing of lots. The annual contingent is known as a class, numbered correspondingly to the number of years' service since enrolment. Thus the 1st class contains the recruits of the current year, the 2nd class those of the previous year, and so on.

(8674)   B

The term of service is 8 years in the active army and 5 years in the reserve. Of the 8 years' army service, however, only a portion is spent with the colours and the remainder on what is termed unlimited leave, which practically corresponds to our reserve service.

The periods of training with the colours in the different arms is actually as follows :—

Infantry : 20 months during the 24 months following their incorporation.

Cavalry and horse artillery : 36 months during the 39 months following their incorporation.

Field artillery and train : 28 months during the 30 months following their incorporation.

Fortress artillery and special companies of artificers, 22 months during the 24 months following their incorporation.

Engineers : 22 months during the 34 months following their incorporation.

Battalion of administration : 24 months continuously.

The Government has the right to recall to the colours any men on unlimited leave. Those who have only performed 20 months' service are liable to recall for 1 month's training during their third or fourth year's service, and all men on unlimited leave or in the reserve have to attend 1 inspection parade annually.

Men belonging to the reserve can only be mobilized in the event of war or of Belgian territory being threatened ; and, further, the 11th, 12th, and 13th classes can only be mobilized in case of absolute necessity, and can then only be employed in the defence of fortresses or in auxiliary services in connection with the army. The Crown may also in case of necessity call out older classes, *e.g.*, the 14th and 15th, but the same limitations apply as to the 3 classes above mentioned.

There are 5 kinds of volunteers with varying conditions of service—

1. *Volontaires de carrière* may enlist between the ages of 16 and 35 (or 40 if they have served before). Their engagement is for at least 13 years, of which 3 are with the colours and the remainder in the reserve. Youths under 18 may enlist, but their service does not count until they reach that age. If before that time they find themselves unsuited for the army, they may be allowed to cancel their engagement and take their chance in the drawing of lots as *miliciens*. *Volontaires de carrière* are allowed to choose the arm of the service in which they wish to serve.

2. *Volontaires du contingent* are young men who are liable to military service, but who, instead of waiting to be drawn with the contingent to which they belong, elect to enlist. Their terms of service are the same as those of the ordinary *milicien*, but they receive in the dismounted branches a slightly higher rate of pay.

3. *Volontaires avec primes* and *remplacants* are 2 classes of substitutes, the former provided by the State and the latter by private arrangement. Their conditions of service are the same as for ordinary soldiers, but they may choose their arm of the service.

4. *Volontaires de réserve* are men who, on completion of their colour service, agree to extend their reserve service by 2 or 4 years, receiving a bounty of £3 in the first case and £6 in the second. They are regarded as belonging to the 2 youngest classes of the reserve, and are consequently available for service with the field army. Their numbers are now limited.

5. *Rengagés* are men who on completion of their colour service re-engage by periods of 2 years up to a limit which is not stated.

To be eligible as a *volontaire* a candidate must be—

(8674)   B 2

(*a*) Of Belgian nationality.

(*b*) Over 16 years of age and not more than 35, unless he has served before, when he may be taken up to 40.

(*c*) Physically equivalent to the standard required for other recruits, and of the height of—

—	Minimum.		Maximum.	
	ft.	ins.	ft.	ins.
For Line Regiments, Chasseurs, Special Companies of Artillery, and Battalion of Administration	5	0	—	
Train	5	2¼	—	
Carabineers	5	3	5	6¼
Chasseurs à cheval	5	4¼	5	5¾
Engineers	5	5	—	
Lancers	5	5½	5	7
Field Artillery	5	5¾	5	7½
Fortress Artillery	5	6	—	
Guides	5	6½	5	7¼
Grenadiers...	5	7	—	

The lowest rate of pay of an infantry soldier is 28 centimes per day. Grenadiers and other arms receive more. Deductions are made from this for messing.

The following sums are issued to men in addition to the regimental pay :—

	Per month.	
	£	*s.*
Dismounted troops	1	0
Mounted troops	1	4
Volontaire du contingent	1	4
Volontaire de carrière (over 18 years of age)	1	8
Re-engaged men		
Corporal	1	12
Sergeants	2	0

OFFICERS AND NON-COMMISSIONED OFFICERS.

Officers are appointed partly by promotion of non-commissioned officers, partly by direct appointment from the military school.

In the cavalry and infantry one-third of the vacancies in the rank of sub-lieutenant is filled by promotion of non-commissioned officers.

Two-thirds are appointed by the King from among pupils of the military school and non-commissioned officers.

In the artillery and engineers two-thirds of the vacancies are given to pupils of the military school, one-third to non-commissioned officers of those arms.

Admission to the military school is by competitive examination, which is open to soldiers serving as well as to civilians.

The course for cavalry and infantry candidates lasts 2 years, for artillery and engineers 4. At the end of the first year a pupil must undertake to serve in the army at least 8 years.

A certain period, fixed by regulation, must be passed in each rank (whether as a commissioned or non-commissioned officer) to qualify for promotion to a higher grade.

Half the vacancies in the ranks of lieutenant and second captain are filled by seniority, half by selection. All promotions to higher ranks are made by selection.

Staff officers form a special corps, which is recruited from among the officers of the different arms of the service who have satisfactorily completed a 3 years' course at the war school, or who have passed the final examination at that establishment without going through the course. Admission to the school is by competitive examination, a certain number of vacancies being allotted to the different arms. Officers must have 5 years' service before being eligible for examination. The course at the school lasts 3 years, after which officers are attached for 10 months to an arm in which they have not previously served. On completion of this period, those who are considered specially fitted for staff employment are attached for a year to the staff of a district or one of the fortified positions, and subsequently for another year to the "Direction Supérieure" of the Staff Corps.

MILITARY STUDENTS.

Special arrangements are made by which students at various universities and schools may continue their studies and at the same time perform certain military duties and drills. Artisans are given facilities for employment in the special companies belonging to the artillery.

RESERVE AND AUXILIARY OFFICERS.

Reserve officers are appointed from among those who contract a voluntary engagement to serve for 8 years in that capacity. After passing an examination they serve in the ranks for 6 months without pay, and provide their own clothing. They are allowed to live out of barracks, and their uniform is of the material worn by *sous-officiers*. After 6 months' service they are examined in military subjects, and if successful are promoted sergeants. After 2 years' satisfactory service in that rank they are tested in their aptitude for the position of sub-lieutenant, and, if considered satisfactory, they are appointed sub-lieutenants in the reserve, and are sent on leave without pay. They are liable to be called up for 1 month's duty per annum. In addition to the above, any non-commissioned officer may be permitted to go up for the examination laid down for an officer of the reserve, which embraces military regulations, organisation, topography, tactics, artillery, fortification, &c.

Officers who retire from the army may also, under certain conditions, be appointed officers of the reserve for a term of 5 years, which may be extended.

Non-commissioned officers of infantry, of good conduct, who, after completion of 8 years' service, are considered fit for the position of *auxiliary* officer, and who satisfy certain conditions as to education and military attainments, may be appointed as such. They engage to serve in that capacity for 5 years.

NUMBERS AVAILABLE.

The strength of the annual contingent, and the numbers of the peace establishment (which includes men with the colours and those on unlimited furlough), are fixed annually by law.

The following is the strength of the Belgian Army, by arms, according to the figures furnished to the Chamber of Deputies by the Minister of War in December, 1905.

Arms.	Officers.		Men.				Total.
	On the Active List.	Reserve.	With the Colours.	On unlimited leave.	Reserve.	Total.	
					Reserve.		
Infantry	1,745	125	22,759	49,174	38,779	87,953	110,712
Cavalry	304	15	5,866	3,707	—	3,707	9,573
Artillery	544	21	8,205	10,655	10,938	21,593	29,798
Engineers	150	13	1,484	2,968	2,356	5,324	6,808
Gendarmerie	67	—	3,069	10	—	10	3,079
Other corps	663	7	2,068	3,529	5,941	9,470	11,538
	3,473	181	43,451	70,043	58,014	128,057	171,508

3,654

Add also —
Officers	3,654
Volontaires de réserve	10,000
Civil officials	1,800
Ecole d'application	101
Bandmasters ranking as officers	13
Officers on half-pay	40
Grand total	187,116

CHAPTER II.

PEACE AND WAR ORGANISATION.

1. PEACE ORGANISATION.

BELGIUM is divided into 4 military districts.

The first district comprises the provinces of East and West Flanders, with headquarters at Ghent.

The second, the province of Antwerp ; headquarters, Antwerp.

The third, the provinces of Limbourg, Liége, and Luxembourg, with headquarters at Liége.

The fourth, the provinces of Brabant, Namur, and Hainault ; headquarters at Brussels.

Each district is commanded by a lieutenant-general, who exercises authority over all troops stationed in his command, without, however, interfering with the special duties of the inspectors general of cavalry, artillery, engineers, hospitals, and intendance. The officer commanding a district carries out all movements of troops ordered by superior authority, and is responsible for the discipline and efficiency in every way of all troops in his command. In war he becomes commander of the corresponding division of the field army, and most of the larger units composing it are quartered in the district in peace time.

At each of the important fortresses, Antwerp, Liége, and Namur, and also at the minor one of Termonde,* there is a defence committee, composed, as a rule, of the general or other officer in command as president,

---

* Termonde is to be dismantled on completion of the new scheme for the defence of Antwerp.

the chief of his staff, the directors of artillery and fortifications of the district, an officer of intendance, and a medical officer. The committee prepare all schemes for the defence of the fortress.

The measures proposed by these committees are supervised by a superior committee of defence, composed of the inspectors-general of artillery and engineers, and the chief of the staff at headquarters.

The Belgian Army in peace consists of the following units, exclusive of reserve battalions, depôts, and general staff :—

58 battalions of infantry and 4 disciplinary companies.
40 squadrons of cavalry.
4 batteries of horse artillery.
30 batteries of field artillery.
51 batteries of fortress artillery and 3 special companies.
1 regiment of engineers and 5 special companies.
1 battalion (7 companies) of train.
1 battalion (4 companies) of administration (supply and hospital services).

2. WAR ORGANISATION.

The system of defence by which Belgium expects to ensure her neutrality is, briefly, to fortify Antwerp as strongly as possible, in view of its being the national *réduit;* to secure the line of the Meuse by holding the fortresses of Liége, Namur, and Huy ; and to put in the field, wherever needed, a field army of about 100,000 men.

The Field Army.

The field army will consist of 4 divisions and 2 cavalry divisions, with one head-quarters staff.

The head-quarters staff of the army is divided into

two portions or "groups." The second furnishes the staff of the line of communications and includes the directors of artillery, engineers, medical and administration services.

In addition to the necessary supply, medical, veterinary and administrative units, the under-mentioned troops are attached to the headquarters staff.

To the 1st "group" :—

       1 railway company of engineers.
       1 pontoon company of engineers.
       1 section field telegraph.

To the 2nd "group" :—

       1 section field telegraph.

The railway and pontoon companies may be eventually transferred to the second "group."

Organisation of a Division of the Field Army.

Composition.—The component parts of a division are—

Divisional staff.
2 active brigades of infantry, each of 2 regiments (6 battalions), and 1 reserve brigade of infantry of 2 regiments (4 battalions).
1 battalion of rifles (belonging to the regiment of carabineers).
1 field company of engineers.
1 regiment of field artillery (8 batteries 1st and 4th divisions, 7 batteries 2nd and 3rd divisions).
1 squadron of gendarmerie.
1 section field telegraph.
2 artillery ammunition columns.
2 infantry   ,,   ,,
1 section engineer park.
1 ambulance column.

1 supply column, with staff and detachment for supply duties.

2 field hospitals.

1 remount depôt.

Strength.—The war strengths of the divisions are :—

—	Officers, N.C.O.'s, and men.	Horses.	Guns.	Vehicles.
1st and 4th	22,715	3,210	48	402
2nd and 3rd... ...	22,543	3,054	42	389

Fighting strength.—Deducting non-combatants and officers and non-commissioned officers not in the ranks, the fighting strength of a division may be taken at :—

18,096 bayonets.

100 sabres.

48 or 42 guns.

Organisation of a Cavalry Division.

Composition.—The component parts of a cavalry division are :—

Divisional staff.

2 brigades of cavalry, each of 2 regiments (10 squadrons).

2 batteries of horse artillery.

1 artillery ammunition column.

1 ambulance column.

Strength.—The war strength of a normal cavalry division, as given above, is :—

Officers, N.C.O.'s, and men.	Horses.	Guns.	Vehicles.
4,112	4,186	12	96

Fighting Strength.—Deducting non-combatants and officers and others not in the ranks, the fighting strength of a cavalry division may be taken at :—

2,700 sabres.
12 guns.

Troops for Fortress Defence and Depôts.

The troops considered necessary for the fortresses are as under :—

Antwerp	...	...	... 56,200
Liége...	...	...	... 15,400
Namur	...	...	... 13,400
Huy ...	...	...	... 2,800
	Total	...	87,800

These numbers will be made up of the following units, in addition to the "Garde Civique" :—

Infantry.

13th and 14th line regiments, comprising 6 active, 2 reserve, and 4 fortress battalions.

1 reserve battalion carabiniers.

8 regiments of fortress infantry (5th and 6th battalions of regiments bearing an even number and grenadiers).

3 fortress battalions carabiniers, forming 1 regiment.

16 separate fortress battalions.

Total infantry—6 active, 3 reserve, and 39 fortress battalions.

Cavalry.

8 reserve squadrons, to be raised in time of war.

Artillery.

6 reserve batteries field artillery.
2 artillery ammunition columns.
15 battalions fortress artillery, comprising 78 batteries.

Engineers.

20 fortress companies.
1 telegraph company.
1 pontoon company.
1 S.M. mining and artificers company,
1 balloon and labourers company.

Medical.

1 ambulance column.

The distribution of units to each fortress is not definitely known, but the 13th and 14th line regiments are assigned to Namur and Liége respectively. The garrisons are organised in two categories: (*a*) for mobile defence, (*b*) for manning fixed defences. The former are found by the fortress battalions which are organised in regiments, and the latter by those constituted separately.

The depôts troops will be distributed among—

19 infantry depôts.
8 cavalry   „
4 field artillery depôts.
3 garrison artillery depôts.
1 engineer   „   „
1 train   „   „

CHAPTER III.

INFANTRY AND CYCLISTS.

1. ORGANISATION.

THE infantry consists of :—

    1 regiment of carabineers.
    1   ,,   grenadiers.
    3 regiments of chasseurs-à-pied.
    14   ,,   the line.

The regiment of carabineers has a staff, 4 active battalions, 1 reserve battalion and 3 fortress battalions. The other regiments have a staff, 3 active battalions, 1 reserve battalion and 2 fortress battalions.

The battalions consist each of a staff and 4 companies. One company in each of the active carabineer battalions is a cyclist company.

Each regiment has a depôt composed of a staff and one company.

There are also :—

    A discipline corps of 4 companies.
    A school for sons of soldiers training for the non-commissioned rank.
    A cadet school.

Only the cadres of the reserve and fortress battalions are kept up in time of peace. On mobilization the active battalions and 16 reserve battalions, completed to war establishment, join the field army (except the 13th and 14th regiments, which are assigned to the defences of Liége and Namur), while the remaining reserve and fortress battalions form the garrisons of the fortresses.

The infantry is organised in 4 divisions, a division consisting of 2 brigades, each of 2 regiments. The 3rd division, in peace time, however, consists of 3 brigades]; the 9th brigade, which includes the 13th and 14th regiments of the line, and is intended for the defences of Liége and Namur, being attached to it. The 8th brigade, in peace, consists of 3 regiments, the carabineer regiment (the 4 active battalions of which, in war, form the divisional rifle battalions) being attached to it. Each battalion consists of four companies, each company of 3 pelotons, each peloton of 2 sections, and each section of 2 squads.

The peace stations of the various units, and the larger units in the field army to which they belong, are shown in Appendix I. Their strengths on a peace and war footing are given below.

Unit.	Peace. Officers.	Peace. N.C.O.'s and men.	Peace. Horses.	Peace. Vehicles.	War. Officers.	War. N.C.O.'s and men.	War. Horses.	War. Vehicles.	Remarks.
Staff of—									
Regiment	5	28	5	—	5	38	10	2	
Active battalion	2	5	2	—	4	20	24	4	
Reserve battalion	1	3	1	—	—	—	—	—	
Fortress battalion	1*	1	1	—	—	—	—	—	* 6th Battalion Carabineers only.
Depôt battalion	2	4	1	—	—	—	—	—	
Corps of discipline	4	10	4	—	—	—	—	—	
Company—									
Active battalion	4	97	—	—	4	260	—	—	† 1 officer in 4th company.
Reserve battalion	2	9	—	—	4	260	—	—	‡ 1 man in 2nd or 4th companies.
Fortress battalion	2†	3 or 4‡	—	—	—	—	—	—	§ Cadets.
Depôt battalion	3	13	—	—	—	—	—	—	‖ Boys.
Corps of discipline	5	29	—	—	—	—	—	—	
Cadet school	—	100§	—	—	—	—	—	—	
Training school	—	450‖	—	—	—	—	—	—	
Battalion—									
Active	18	393	2	—	20¶	1,060	24	4	¶ Except Carabineers.
Reserve	9	39	1	—	20	1,060	24	4	
Fortress	8	10	1	—	—	—	—	—	
Depôt	5	17	1	—	—	—	—	—	
Regiment—									
Carabineers	113	1,685	16	—	65	3,218	82	14	
Grenadiers	87	1,282	13	—	—	—	—	—	
Line									
Chasseurs									

Uniform.

(A) *Infantry of the Line.*

Tunic.—Dark blue, double breasted, with scarlet collar, and scarlet wool "wings" (yellow for drummers and buglers).

Undress jacket.—Dark blue, single breasted (worn by corporals and privates only).

Trousers.—Blue grey, with scarlet piping.

Shako.—Dark blue felt, with scarlet trimmings and ball tuft (except for bandsmen, who wear a drooping plume of white swan's feathers).

Forage cap.—Circular, dark blue, with scarlet band, and number of regiment in front.

Greatcoat.—Dark blue, double-breasted.

Tunics, epaulettes and lines, and plumes, are not taken on service.

Officers

Wear the same as the men, but with a broad scarlet stripe on each side of the piping on the trousers, and badges of rank on collar. The forage cap is of different pattern, like a low shako, after the French pattern.

In full dress, officers wear a crimson silk sash round the waist, and wear epaulettes, and, for regimental staff, white vultures' plumes in the shako, and an aigrette for a colonel or lieutenant-colonel commanding.

(B) *Chasseurs-à-pied.*

Uniform as for the line, with the following exceptions:—

Tunic.—Dark green with collar of the same colour, and light green "wings." "Lines" of yellow wool (in full dress).

Undress jacket.—Dark green.

Trousers.—Belgian grey, with yellow piping.

Shako.—Dark green, light green trimmings, and black plume of cock's feathers.

Forage cap.—Dark green, with yellow band.

Greatcoat.—Dark green.

Officers.

As the men, with the exceptions peculiar to officers noted above. Officers of chasseurs, however, do not wear epaulettes, and their "lines" are of gold lace. Their plumes are black : vulture for staff, cock's feathers for other ranks.

(C) *Grenadiers.*

As for the line, with the following exceptions :—

Trousers.—Dark blue, with broad scarlet stripe.

Bearskin caps instead of shakos.

Grenades are worn on corners of collars, and, in full dress, epaulettes of scarlet wool.

Officers.

As the men, with the same difference as for the line. Officers of grenadiers, however, wear gold lace "lines" in full dress. Plumes : vulture, white for staff, red for company officers.

(D) *Carabineers.*

The same uniform as for chasseurs-à-pied, except the head-dress, which is a black felt hat of special shape, with a brim, and plume of black cock's feathers on the left side.

In drill order and service order ("tenue de campagne") officers and men wear leather gaiters.

(8674)   c 2

ARMAMENT.

Officers.—Browning pistol, and sword with steel scabbard.

Sergeant-majors ("adjudants-sous-officiers").—Revolver. Sword with leather scabbard.

Off duty, certain non-commissioned officers holding ranks analogous to that of staff-sergeants wear a sword similar to the above.

Sergeants.—All wear, off duty, a sword bayonet of special pattern.

Bandsmen wear a sword of special pattern, with black leather scabbard.

Other ranks are armed with Mauser repeating rifle and sword bayonet. For details, *see* Chapter X.

EQUIPMENT.

The new pattern equipment of an infantry soldier consists of a knapsack with braces, cloak-straps, mess-tin (or cooking-pot) strap, collapsible bucket, waist-belt, ammunition pouch, haversack, water bottle, and entrenching tool.

The knapsack is of raw cowhide on a wicker-work frame. The lower part forms a box for carrying rations. On each outer side of the knapsack is a pocket for ammunition. The braces pass over the shoulders and back, under the arms, to the bottom of the knapsack, and the weight is also taken by short supporting straps to each side of the ammunition pouch, which is worn on the belt in front of the centre of the body. Belts and pouches are of black leather. In peace time the greatcoat may be rolled over the top and down each side of the knapsack and fastened by its four straps. On service it is always worn on the person. The cooking-pot is strapped to the flap of the knapsack. The haversack or wallet is carried, by means of runners, on the waistbelt, and the water bottle hooked on to the exterior side of the haversack and kept in place by a loop in which it rests. A detachable belt is also provided to enable the haversack to be carried over the shoulder when the waistbelt is not worn. The entrenching tool (spade or billhook) is carried in its carriage on the waistbelt and kept steady by attachment to the bayonet. If a hand-saw is carried it is placed under the flap of the knapsack. The two pockets for ammunition are intended to hold 30 rounds each (2 packets of 15), and the ammunition pouch will, as a rule, contain 60 rounds, though 100 may be carried.

Although the equipment described above is now the regulation pattern, the old pattern is to be worn out. The principal differences are that the old pattern knapsack is heavier, being made of wood instead of wicker-work. It has no pockets for ammunition, the greatcoat is rolled on the top, the water bottle is hooked to the waistbelt, and the entrenching tool generally carried suspended at the left side by a strap passing over the right shoulder.

Three orders of dress are recognised throughout the service :—

      (a) Full dress.
      (b) Undress.
      (c) Marching or service order.

Every soldier on mobilization will receive a description card ("plaque d'identité"), and a field dressing ("sachet de pansement") containing lint and a bandage. Pockets are provided for these, that for the field dressing being on the inside of the left breast of the greatcoat for dismounted, and of the jacket for mounted services.

Military Cyclists.

One company in each of the four carabineer battalions is a cyclist company.

The drill is based on the English " Drill of a Cyclist Section." A very complete course of training (both military and physical) was instituted in the cyclist school originally organised in the carabineer regiment, and the cyclists received training not only in riding and drill, but in map-reading, reconnaissance, reports, and other duties in the field ; in the mechanism, care, and repair of their machines ; and in carrying verbal messages and orders.

The cycle now used is the " Belgica," a folding portable machine manufactured by M. Mettewie in Belgium.

CHAPTER IV.

CAVALRY.

ORGANISATION.

THE Belgian cavalry consists of :—

    2 regiments of chasseurs-à-cheval.
    2   „   „ guides.
    4   „   „ lancers.

These are combined in divisions and brigades as follows :—

1st Division.

1st Brigade.	2nd Brigade.
1st Guides.	1st Lancers.
2nd „	2nd „

2nd Division.

3rd Brigade.	4th Brigade.
1st Chasseurs-à-cheval.	3rd Lancers.
2nd „	4th „

Each regiment in peace time consists of regimental staff, 5 squadrons, and a depôt squadron.

On mobilization an additional squadron is added, making a total of 6 squadrons and a depôt squadron.

Of these, 5 squadrons are included in each regiment of the field army. The 6th squadron of each regiment is attached to the mobile troops for fortress defence.

The peace stations of the various regiments are shown in Appendix I. Their establishments are given below :—

CAVALRY ESTABLISHMENTS.

Unit.	Peace.			War.			
	Officers.	N.C.O.'s and men.	Horses.	Officers.	N.C.O.'s and men.	Horses.	Vehicles.
Staff of a regiment ...	9	9	27	7	17	25	1
Squadron, active ...	5	130	130	5	165	170	2
,, depôt ...	4	12	15	—	—	—	—
Regiment (Staff, 5 squadrons and depôt)	38	671	692	36	846	885	11

UNIFORMS.

The shape of the uniform (except full dress head-dress) is the same for all cavalry. The distinctive colours, &c., are as follows :—

(A) *Chasseurs-à-Cheval.*

Jacket.—Dark blue with white braid, except for trumpeters, who wear, in the first regiment, yellow braid, in the 2nd regiment, scarlet.

Undress jacket.—As for infantry, but with yellow collar and piping in the 1st regiment, scarlet in the 2nd regiment.

Cloak.—Dark blue with cape attached.

Overalls.—Blue grey with white stripes.

Shako.—Same shape as infantry. 1st regiment blue, 2nd regiment scarlet. White trimmings and white horsehair plume.

Forage cap —French pattern, dark blue with yellow braid for 1st regiment, scarlet for 2nd regiment.

Officers.

Same as the men, with the following exceptions :—
The lace on the jacket is gold (black braid in undress).
Stripes on overalls, blue.   Shako trimmings, gold.
Plumes : cock's feathers ; for field officers, vulture ; colonel, an aigrette.
The forage cap is of the same pattern as for infantry, but on the march, &c., and on service, officers may wear a forage cap of same shape, &c., as the men.

(B) *Guides.*

Jacket.—Green with yellow braid (for trumpeters and band, magenta).
Undress jacket.—Green, magenta piping.
The number of the regiment is worn on the collar.
Cloak.—Green.
Overalls.—Magenta, yellow stripes.
Busby.—Black bearskin ; busby bag, magenta ; plume, white.
Forage cap.—Green, with magenta piping and yellow braid.

Officers.

Same as the men, but with gold lace instead of yellow braid (black braid in undress), green stripes instead of yellow on the overalls, &c.   Forage cap as for chasseurs, but green.

(C) *Lancers.*

The uniform is the same as for chasseurs (lancer cap excepted) with the following regimental distinctions :—

	Braid on jacket.		Lancer cap.	Plume.*
—	Men.	Trumpeters.		
1st Lancers ...	White	Crimson	Crimson	White.
2nd ,, ...	White	Yellow	Yellow	White.
3rd ,, ...	Yellow	White	White	Scarlet.
4th ,, ...	Yellow	Sky Blue	Sky Blue	Scarlet.

* Horse-hair for men, cock's feathers for officers, vulture for field officers, an aigrette for colonel.

Stripes of overalls and } 1st and 2nd, white.
braid on forage cap } 3rd and 4th, yellow.

Officers.

The same as officers of chasseurs, except as regards the lancer cap, which is the same as the men, but with gold trimmings, &c.

The regulation dress when mounted, for all ranks, is the booted overall, but officers are allowed to wear pantaloons and knee boots, except in marching order and in full dress.

ARMAMENT.

Chasseurs and Guides.

Officers, non-commissioned officers and trumpeters.— Sword and Browning pistol.

Men.—Sword and Mauser repeating carbine. The latter is slung over the left shoulder. The former is carried on the saddle.

Lancers.

Same as the above, with the addition for the rank and file of the lance with pennon of the national colours, which is rolled up in the field.

EQUIPMENT.

The kit is carried in 2 wallets in front of the saddle and a sort of valise with 2 large pockets or wallets, somewhat after the manner of saddle bags, behind the saddle. On the top of the valise is strapped the cloak.

Every man armed with a carbine carries 3 packets of ammunition of 5 rounds each, 1 in each wallet and 1 in a pocket of his jacket, and every man armed with a revolver, 3 boxes containing 6 rounds each, 1 in each wallet and 1 in the revolver case.

CHAPTER V.

ARTILLERY.

ORGANISATION.

THE field artillery consists of 4 regiments.

The first and third regiments of artillery each consist of 8 active and 1 reserve batteries, a depôt, and 1 reserve battery forming the nucleus of 3 artillery ammunition columns.

The second and fourth regiments are each composed of 7 active field and 2 horse batteries, 2 reserve field batteries, a depôt, and a reserve battery forming the nucleus of 3 artillery ammunition columns.

The cadres only of the reserve batteries are maintained in peace time.

The field and horse artillery batteries are numbered throughout from 1 to 40.

On mobilization the 4 regiments of field artillery and the horse artillery batteries are assigned to the 4 divisions of the field army and the 2 cavalry divisions, while the 6 reserve field batteries will join the troops for mobile fortress defence.

The battery is, speaking generally, the tactical and administrative unit of the artillery.

Field batteries are grouped into brigades ("groupes") of 2 or 3 batteries each. Thus every regiment consists of 3 brigades, each commanded by a major.

The fortress artillery consists of :—

(a) The Antwerp batteries (30 active, 20 reserve, and a depôt). The active and reserve batteries are grouped in 8 battalions.

(b) The Liége batteries (12 active, 4 reserve, and a depôt). The active and reserve batteries form 4 battalions.

(c) The Namur batteries (9 active, 3 reserve, and a depôt). The active and reserve batteries are grouped in 3 battalions.

The peace strength of each of the Antwerp batteries is 3 officers and 55 men, and of the Liége and Namur batteries 3 officers and 75 men.

Special Companies.

In addition to the above there are three special companies ; a laboratory company, a company of artificers, and a company of armourers.

The laboratory company is employed in the manufacture of munitions of war at Antwerp.

The company of artificers is employed in the arsenal, at Antwerp, in the construction and repair of gun-carriages, wagons, &c., and in training artificers for field batteries.

The company of armourers is employed in the manufacture of arms at Liége. It supplies armourers for all regiments.

Ammunition Columns.

The cadres only of ammunition columns are maintained in peace time. In war, 12 artillery ammunition columns will be formed, numbered from 1 to 12. Nos. 5 and 10 are horse artillery ammunition columns for 7·5 cm. guns, and will be attached to the 2 cavalry divisions. The remainder are for the 5 army divisions.

The infantry ammunition columns (10 in number, viz., 2 for each division of the field army and 2 for the fifth division) are furnished by the train regiment, supplemented by infantry detachments.

The establishments of all artillery units, and of the special companies, are given on the page opposite.

ARTILLERY ESTABLISHMENTS.

Unit.	Peace.			War.				
	Officers	N.C.O.'s and men.	Horses.	Officers.	N.C.O.'s and men.	Horses.	Guns.	Other vehicles.
Special Services (Staff) ...	72	117	29	●	—	—	—	—
Staff—								
Field artillery regiment	10* or 12†	8	21* or 24†	5	13	15	—	1
Field artillery group ...	—	—	—	3	7	14	—	1
Horse artillery group ...	—	—	—	5	6	10	—	—
Ammunition columns	—	—	—	5	12	16	—	1
Battery—								
Horse artillery ...	4	114	107	5	181 or 180	217 or 216	6	13
Field artillery ...	4	97	61	5	168 or 169	157 or 158	6	13
Reserve field artillery	3	18	13	—	—	—	—	—
Field artillery‡ ammunition column	5 or 6	14	13 or 14	3	112	132	—	18
Horse artillery ammunition column§	—	—	—	3	78	92	—	12
Depôt ...	2	16	8	—	—	—	—	—

* 1st and 3rd Regiments.
† 2nd and 4th Regiment.
‡ For Infantry ammunition column, *see* Train Establishment, p. 48.
§ Formed on 1st day of mobilization.

ARTILLERY ESTABLISHMENTS—*continued.*

32

Unit.	Peace. Officers.	Peace. N.C.O.'s and men.	Peace. Horses.	War. Officers.	War. N.C.O.'s and men.	War. Horses.	War. Guns.	War. Other vehicles.
Fortress artillery—								
Staff of Antwerp defences	20	22	25	—	—	—	—	—
Staff of Liége defences	8	7	10	—	—	—	—	—
Staff of Namur defences	7	7	9	—	—	—	—	—
Battery of Antwerp defences ...	3	55	—	—	—	—	—	—
Battery of Liége and Namur defences	3	75	—	—	—	—	—	—
Battery, reserve	1	4	—	—	—	—	—	—
Depôt	2	17	25	—	—	—	—	—
Total Antwerp defences (8 battalions, 1 depôt)	132	1,771	—	—	—	—	—	—
Total Liége defences (4 battalions, 1 depôt)	50	940	10	—	—	—	—	—
Total Namur defences (3 battalions, 1 depôt)	39	711	9	—	—	—	—	—
Special companies—								
Laboratory company	4	47	—	—	—	—	—	—
Company of armourers	4	47	—	—	—	—	—	—
Company of artificers	4	55	—	—	—	—	—	—

Uniform.

Dark blue, scarlet facings.

Tunic.—In full dress a "coatee," single breasted, with short skirts and epaulettes as for grenadiers, is worn, and, in field and horse batteries, a pouch belt.

Undress jacket.—As for infantry, but with shoulder straps on which is the number of the regiment. Fortress artillery wear the letter A, L, or N,* instead of numbers.

Cloak.—Field and horse artillery wear a dark blue cloak of cavalry pattern, but with the number of the regiment on the corners of the collar.

Greatcoat.—Fortress artillery wear a greatcoat of infantry pattern with the letter A, L, or N on the collar.

Trousers and Overalls.— Dark grey, with broad red stripe.

Head-dress.— Field and horse artillery wear a busby, with scarlet busby-bag and scarlet and black plume.

Fortress artillery wear a shako as for infantry, but with plate of regimental pattern and black horsehair plume.

Lines, of scarlet wool, are worn.

Forage Cap.—Cavalry pattern, dark blue and scarlet, with grenade in front.

Officers.

Same as the men, except that epaulettes and lines are of gold ; plumes for fortress artillery are of black cock's feathers, and for staff of field artillery black and white, instead of black and red, and for staff of fortress artillery black vulture's, instead of cock's, feathers.

---

* Antwerp, Liége, or Namur.

(8674)   D

All officers wear the cavalry pattern cloak and pouch belts and an undress tunic, as for infantry of the line, but with dark blue collar and without collar badges of rank.

Forage cap.—As for infantry of the line.

ARMAMENT.

*Field artillery are armed with the 8·7 cm. (3·42-inch) Krupp B.L. gun, and

Horse artillery with the 7·5 cm. (2·95-inch) Krupp B.L. gun. (For details, *see* Chapter X.)

Field and horse artillery.—Dismounted men carry swords (old infantry pattern) worn in a frog on the belt.

Mounted men, sword of cavalry pattern, with waist-belt and slings (on service the sword is carried on the saddle).

Drivers, gunners, artificers, and shoeing-smiths of horse artillery, and drivers, artificers, and shoeing-smiths of field artillery are armed in peace with sword and revolver, but on mobilization the sword is returned to store.

Non-commissioned officers and trumpeters carry in addition a revolver as for cavalry.

Fortress artillery.—Non-commissioned officers carry the " sabre de sortie " scabbard with leather belt and single sling. The men are armed with the Albini rifle, an antiquated breechloader, which is to be replaced by the Mauser carbine (1905). Corporals and men of the first class carry a bayonet in walking-out dress and on duty without arms.

All officers carry a sword and Browning pistol.

---

* The field artillery is to be re-armed with the 7·5 cm. Q.F. Krupp gun.

EQUIPMENT.

Dismounted men have a similar equipment to infantry, and mounted men to cavalry, though the artillery appear to use an older pattern than the cavalry.

Saddlery, &c., for officers is as for cavalry officers.

CHAPTER VI.

ENGINEERS.

THE corps of engineers consists of :—

(a) A special staff, which includes a number of civilians.

(b) A regiment, comprising a staff, 6 battalions and a depôt. Each battalion consists of a staff and 4 companies, composed as under:—

First Battalion (field) has 4 active companies.

Second „ (fortress) has 4 „ „

Third and Fourth Battalions (fortress) have 2 active and 2 reserve companies.

Fifth and Sixth Battalions (fortress) have 4 reserve companies.

On mobilization the companies of the First Battalion are allotted to the divisions of the field army, while those of the remainder go to make up the garrison of Antwerp, Liége, and Namur.

The depôt consists of a staff and 1 company.

(c) Five special companies, viz. :—

1 telegraph company.

1 submarine mining and artificers company.

1 railway company.

1 pontoon company.

1 labourer and balloonist company.

On mobilization the telegraph company forms 6 sections of field telegraphists, one of which is attached to each division of the field army. The remaining 2 sections, together with the railway and pontoon companies, are attached to the head-quarters staff of the field army. The labourer and balloonist company furnishes the personnel for the engineer park attached to each division.

The active companies composed of the youngest

ENGINEER ESTABLISHMENTS.

Unit.	Peace.				War.			
	Officers.	N.C.O.'s and men.	Civilians.	Horses.	Officers.	N.C.O.'s and men.	Horses.	Vehicles.
Special Staff	65	—	190	25	—	—	—	—
Regimental Staff	3	4	—	5	—	—	—	—
Battalion Staff of 1st, 2nd, 3rd and 4th battalions	2	2	—	2	—	—	—	—
Depôt Staff	2	5	—	1	—	—	—	—
Field company— Active (1st battalion)	4	92	—	—	6	267	31	5
Fortress company— Active (2nd, 3rd and 4th battalions) ...	4	77	—	—	—	—	—	—
Reserve (3rd, 4th, 5th and 6th battalions)	1	2	—	—	—	—	—	—
Depôt company	3	13	—	5	—	—	—	—
Telegraph company...	5	115	—	—	1	58	18	4
Section field telegraphists* (formed 1st day of mobilization)	—	—	—	—	—	—	—	—
Submarine mining and artificer company	4	83	—	—	—	—	—	—
Railway company	4	83	—	5	—	—	—	—
Pontoon company	5	115	—	—	—	—	—	—
Labourers and balloon company ...	5	115	—	—	—	—	—	—

* Including detachment of train.

classes of militia are assigned to the field army, the reserve companies to the Antwerp defences.

The peace and war strengths of the various engineer units are given below.

Their peace stations will be found in Appendix I.

Uniforms.

Tunic.—As for grenadiers, but with black collar and facings.

Undress jacket.—As for grenadiers, but with black collar and facings.

Greatcoat.—As for infantry of the line, but with regimental badge on the corners of the collar.

Trousers.—Dark blue, with broad scarlet stripe as for grenadiers.

Shako.—As for infantry of the line, but with regimental badges and black plume of cock's feathers.

Forage cap.—A sort of small shako of dark blue cloth with scarlet trimmings.

Officers.

The dress of officers is in all respects similar to that of officers of infantry of the line, except that collars and facings are of black velvet and plumes are black.

The civil establishment wear a uniform similar to that of other engineer officers, but with special badges of rank, and wear cocked hats.

Armament and Equipment.

All ranks the same as infantry of the line.

CHAPTER VII.

DEPARTMENTAL SERVICES.

All duties connected with supply are performed by the Administrative Services, which comprise—

(i) The Intendance.
(ii) The Administrative Officers of Corps.
(iii) The Battalion of Aministration.

(i) *The Intendance.*

The Intendance is an administrative corps specially charged with the direction and control of all matters in connection with army funds, pay, clothing, hospitals, and supply services of all kinds. The *executive* duties in connection with these are carried out under the supervision of officers of intendance by paymasters and quartermasters of corps and by the battalion of administration.

Officers of the Intendance are appointed from—

(*a*) Administrative officers of corps.
(*b*) Captains of all arms and officers of the battalion of administration holding the rank of captain.

The peace establishment of the corps is as follows :—

1 chief intendant, with rank of major-general.
4 first-class intendants, with rank of colonel.
6 second-class intendants, with rank of lieut.-colonel.

13 first-class sub-intendants, with rank of major.
9 second-class sub-intendants, with rank of captain-commandant.
6 third-class sub-intendants, with rank of second-captain.

The chief intendant performs the duties of director of administration at the Ministry of War.

The remainder of the officers are distributed at the Ministry of War and among the 4 military districts.

They are charged with the supervision of all supply services, hospitals, and the auditing of accounts.

On mobilization the corps will be augmented to a strength of 60 officers.

The administrative services of the various parts of the field army are under the direct authority of their commanders. The direction and responsibility of these services are entrusted to the officers of intendance attached to army headquarters and to the headquarters of divisions, &c.

Uniform.

The chief intendant wears the uniform of a major-general, but without epaulettes and with slight differences in shoulder cords and sash.

Other officers.—Uniform of usual infantry pattern with scarlet piping, and in full dress gold-laced trousers and "lines" as for chasseurs-à-pied, and green and gold sash round the waist. Cocked hat.

(ii) *Administrative Officers of Corps.*

To every regiment are attached administrative officers charged with accounts generally, payment, and clothing of the men.

The establishment in peace time comprises—

40 first captains (quartermasters), including 1 for
  gendarmerie.
19 second captains (paymasters).
57 lieutenants and sub-lieutenants (paymasters).
39 captains for clothing duties, including 1 for
  gendarmerie.

Officers are usually appointed in the first instance
as sub-lieutenants for pay duties, after passing the
prescribed examination. Half the vacancies are
given to sub lieutenants of all arms, and to the
fourth-class officers of the battalion of administration ;
half to non-commissioned officers. Certain vacancies
in the higher grades are open to other officers after
passing an examination.

On mobilization the establishment will be increased
to 216 officers of all grades to meet the requirements
of reserve regiments, &c.

Uniform.

Similar to that of officers of the intendance, with
regimental buttons.

(iii) *The Battalion of Administration.*

The supply of food and forage, the *personnel*
(exclusive of officers) and requirements of the medical,
veterinary, and chaplains departments are furnished
by the battalion of administration, which comprises a
staff and 4 companies. Each company is organised in
6 sections, viz., bakery, butchery, forage, hospital,
veterinary, and chaplains section.

The peace strength of the battalion for 1906 is
78 officers, 482 non-commissioned officers and men ;
on mobilization it would be raised to a strength of
97 officers, 3,391 non-commissioned officers and men.

The strength and composition of the various units
furnished by the Battalion of Administration are given
on p. 43.

There is attached to the battalion a small section (*section du service judiciaire*) for legal and clerical duties in connection with courts-martial, &c., also a section of staff clerks (*secrétaires-archivistes*).

Officers of the battalion of administration are non-combatants. They are of 5 grades.

The vacancies are given partly to sub-lieutenants and lieutenants of all arms, and partly to non-commissioned officers of the battalion, after passing the prescribed examination.

A central army clothing establishment has been organised since 1904. It is charged with the provision of all material required for, and with the manufacture of all clothing, boots, and necessaries for the troops.

Regimental master tailors and shoemakers will be gradually abolished.

Uniform.

Similar to that of infantry of the line, but with sky-blue trimmings, &c., and dark blue trousers.

Officers wear cocked hats.

Armament.

Officers.—As for infantry.

Sergeants carry the " yatagan " as in the infantry.

Corporals and soldiers carry the " sabre briquet " infantry sword, except the bakery sections, which are armed with carbine and bayonet.

Administrative Services.

Establishments.

Unit.	Peace.			War.			
	Officers.	N.C.O.'s and men.	Horses.	Officers.	N.C.O.'s and men.	Horses.	Vehicles.
Intendance	39	—	20	—	—	—	—
Administrative officers of corps ...	155	—	—	—	—	—	—
Battalion of Administration—							
Staff	7	29	—	—	—	—	—
Judicial section	—	14	—	—	—	—	—
Staff clerk section... ...	—	78	—	—	—	—	—
Bakery section	17	24	—	—	—	—	—
Butchery section ...	14	55	—	—	—	—	—
Forage section	16	24	—	—	—	—	—
Hospital section * ...	24	254	—	—	—	—	—
Veterinary section ...	—	4	—	—	—	—	—
Chaplains section ...	Unpaid reservists.			—	—	—	—
Supply detachment† ...	Formed on first day of mobilization.			2	79	8	2
Field hospital‡ ...				7	39	23	5

* In addition to unpaid reservists.   † Including details from train.

† Including medical and train details.

Medical and Veterinary Services.

The medical department consists in peace time of 210 medical and 41 veterinary officers, which numbers will be raised on mobilization to 362 medical and 49 veterinary officers.

The distribution of the medical *personnel* and allotment to units is given below.

—	Peace.		War.		
	Officers.	Horses.	Officers.	N.C.O.'s and men.	Horses.
Medical services—*					
For hospital duties	94	2	—	—	—
For regimental duties ...	116	26	—	—	—
With ambulance column ⎱ of field army divisions†			3	18	—
With ambulance column ⎰ of cavaly divisions†	Formed on first day of mobilization.		3	2	2
With each field hospital‡			5	2	1

* These figures denote medical personnel only.
　† For complete establishment of ambulance columns, *see* Train Establishments, p. 48.
　‡ For complete establishment of field hospitals, *see* Administrative Services Establishments, p. 43.

The *personnel* of the lower ranks for the different medical units is found on mobilization, as already stated, by the battalion of administration.

The medical services in war time are further supplemented by the assistance rendered by the Red Cross Society of Belgium, which acts under the orders of the military medical officers.

The care of the wounded on the field of battle is organised as follows :—

(1) "*Service de la ligne de combat*"—comprising collection of, and first aid to, the wounded, and despatch to the

(2) "*Poste de secours*"—of which the primary object is to put the wounded as, rapidly as possible in a state to admit of their being transported to the

(3) "*Place de pansement*"—or headquarters of the ambulance column. This is the centre of medical aid for a division.

(4) *Field hospitals.*—These are intended to reinforce, and act as temporary echelons in rear of, the ambulance columns, and for the despatch of the sick and wounded to regular hospitals.

The arrangements for (1) and (2) are made by regimental surgeons and stretcher bearers ; those for (3) by the ambulance column assisted by regimental surgeons under orders of the divisional medical officer.

All hospital establishments, whether fixed or moveable, fly the national ensign and the flag of the Geneva Convention. By night their position is indicated by lanterns with the Red Geneva Cross. All employed, except regimental stretcher bearers, wear armlets with the Geneva Cross.

UNIFORM.

The *inspector-general*, who holds the rank of major-general, wears the uniform of a general officer (*see* Chapter IX), but without epaulettes in full dress, and with slight differences in shoulder cords and sash.

Other officers.—Similar to that of infantry of the line, but without epaulettes, and with the following differences : facings, &c., magenta for surgeons, light green for dispensers (*pharmaciens*). Dark blue

trousers without stripe—except in full dress. Cocked
hat. A cross belt, with departmental badge, is worn.

ARMAMENT.

As for officers of infantry. Special sword knot.

Train.

Transport for all services of the army is furnished
by the Train, which comprises a staff, 7 companies and
a depôt. It receives a proportion of the annual contingent of *miliciens*, those accustomed to horses and
outdoor work being selected. Its peace strength is
29 officers and 290 non-commissioned officers and men.
On mobilization this will be raised, by the incorporation of its own classes and all available men of the
7th, 8th, 9th, 10th, 11th, 12th and 13th classes of
cavalry reservists, to an establishment of 80 officers
and 5,370 non-commissioned officers and men.

The officers of the regiment are selected from
among the non-commissioned officers of the corps and
from those of cavalry and artillery who have passed
the prescribed examination.

Four companies furnish the transport required for
all units of the four divisions of the field army, 1 for
the 5th division, 1 for the cavalry divisions, 1 for the
head-quarters staff and units attached thereto.

The establishments of the train units are given
on p. 48.

UNIFORM.

Tunic.—As for infantry of the line, but with sky-
blue facings, &c., white buttons, and white shoulder
cords.

Undress jacket.—As for artillery, but with sky-blue
piping.

Cloak.—As for field artillery.

Trousers and booted overalls.—Dark grey, with sky-blue stripe.

Shako.—As for fortress artillery, with black plume, and sky-blue trimmings, &c.

Forage cap.—Cavalry pattern.

Officers.

No special differences beyond those usual in other arms between officers and men. Lace and embroidery are of silver, and a cross belt is worn.

ARMAMENT.

Officers.—As for artillery.

Sergeant-majors.—Sword and revolver.

Non-commissioned officers and trumpeters.—Sword with steel scabbard.

Other ranks.—Carbine (Comblain).

Train Establishments.

Unit.	Peace.			War.			
	Officers.	N.C.O.'s and men.	Horses.	Officers.	N.C.O.'s and men.	Horses.	Vehicles.
Staff	4	5	8	—	—	—	—
Company	3	36 to 40	42 to 53	—	—	—	—
Depôt	4	27	10	—	—	—	—
Infantry ammunition column				3*	137*	178	26
Ambulance columns of field army division				6†	323†	75 to 77	23
Ambulance column of cavalry division	Formed on first day of mobilization.			4‡	33‡	30	6
Supply park				2§	66§	99	23
Supply column				2§	92§	140	32
Remount depôt				3	25	48	1

* Including infantry details.
† Including details from infantry, medical services, and battalion of administration.
‡ Including details from medical services and battalion of administration,
§ Including details from battalion of administration.

CHAPTER VIII.

GENDARMERIE AND CIVIC GUARD.

GENDARMERIE.

THE establishment of the corps of gendarmerie consists of :—

        1 major-general, or colonel.
        1 lieutenant-colonel.
        3 majors.
       11 captains commandant.
       11 2nd captains.
       20 lieutenants.
       20 sub-lieutenants.
        2 captains (quartermaster and officer for clothing duties).
        1 medical officer.
        1 veterinary officer.
    3,075 non-commissioned officers and gendarmes (of whom about 1,765 are cavalry, and 1,310 infantry), and
    1,843 horses.

The corps is organised in a staff and 9 companies. It is under the orders of the War Minister as regards matters connected with discipline, pay, promotion, dress, remounts, and *matériel,* and under the department of the Minister of Justice as regards matters connected with public order, and the exercise of authority as civil police.

(8674)   E

In war the corps furnishes one squadron to each division as divisional cavalry.

Enlistment is for 6 years. All unmarried men, or widowers without children, between the ages of 21 and 35 (or 40 if the candidate has already served), and fulfilling certain conditions as to physique, education, and character, are eligible.

Re-engagements for 2 or 4 years are permitted.

UNIFORM.

As for grenadiers, but of better quality, and with the following differences :—

The tunic is single-breasted, and there is no scarlet stripe on trousers. There are no epaulettes, but aiguillettes are worn by all ranks, of silver for officers, white cotton for other ranks.

Cloaks are of cavalry pattern.

Non-commissioned officers and men have a képi as well as a cavalry forage cap, but of dark blue with white (or silver) braid.

Officers' lace is silver.

ARMAMENT.

Mounted men.—Straight sword, heavy cavalry pattern ; light pattern cavalry carbine, carried slung over the left shoulder ; pistol 1877 pattern.

Dismounted men.—Mauser repeating carbine, model 1889 and yataghan, model 1889, with leather scabbard.

Officers.—Sword and revolver.

CIVIC GUARD.

The Civic Guard, a constitutional force, is active in towns having a population of more than 10,000, and in fortresses ; and is non-active in other communities, except by a special law.

It is charged with the maintenance of order, and the preservation of the independence and integrity of the State.

It is organised by "communes" or groups of "communes," and there are 4 superior districts, each under a lieutenant-general of civic guard, the whole being under an inspector-general who is a retired lieutenant-general. The force is under the orders of the Minister of the Interior, whose authority is exercised through the civil governors and burgomasters. Every male inhabitant between the ages of 20 and 32, who is able to provide himself with the required uniform, is liable to serve in the 1st Ban, and from 33 to 40 in the 2nd, exemption being only allowed in the case of active military service, certain civil functionaries, ministers of religion, and on medical grounds.

Officers not belonging to companies, or similar units, are nominated by the king ; company officers and non-commissioned officers, except the sergeant-major, are elected by the men composing the unit. The force has its own courts-martial for purposes of discipline.

The active portion of the "Garde Civique" is estimated at about 40,708 men.

The men in the active portion receive the following training :—

1st Ban.

1st year.—Before being incorporated in his unit every man must undergo 30 drills of not less than 2 hours' duration, and be passed as efficient, or undergo a second course of 30 drills.

For the remainder of the period of service in the 1st Ban, the men are liable to perform 6 drills per annum, each of 2 hours, and during the first 4 years after their incorporation they may be called out annually for a period of not more than 5 days for company and battalion drills, so arranged as to allow of the men returning to their homes every night.

2nd Ban.

Men of the 2nd Ban may be called upon to perform 3 drills annually of not less than 2 hours' duration. If they have not served in the 1st Ban (*e.g.*, in case of a man who changes his residence from a place where there is no active " Garde Civique " to a place where it is active) they must perform 10 drills in the first year.

An annual inspection is held by commanders of " communes " of all the units under their command.

Special Companies and Corps of the " Garde Civique."—There are 33 companies of " chasseurs-à-pied " distributed in various localities, of which 4 battalions (12 companies) are at Brussels, ½ battalion at Ghent, and 1 battalion at Liége. There are 17 batteries and 11 companies of artillery, the bulk of whom are at Brussels, Antwerp, Ghent, and Liége, 3 companies of " sapeurs-pompiers," and 4 squadrons of " chasseurs-à-cheval." These are formed of volunteers from the civic guard, and are frequently drilled and fairly efficient.

CHAPTER IX.

UNIFORM OF GENERAL AND STAFF OFFICERS, AND BADGES OF RANK.

GENERAL officers wear in full dress a coatee of blue cloth embroidered with gold, with epaulettes and sash (red and gold for lieutenant-generals, black and gold for major-generals); cocked hats are worn and gold-laced trousers when dismounted, white pantaloons and long boots in mounted order.

In undress a double-breasted tunic with gold shoulder cords and crimson piping, &c., is worn, and forage cap of usual pattern; when dismounted dark blue trousers, with stripe of the same colour are worn; when mounted, dark blue pantaloons.

The uniform of the general staff is of dark green, with magenta pipings, &c., and magenta stripe on trousers, &c. Shako as for infantry, of the line, of dark green with gold lace and shako lines, and white plumes. Forage cap as for infantry, of dark green. Epaulettes and sash as for infantry, but the sash is worn over the left shoulder. On service the shako is worn with a cover and without plume. Staff officers carry sword and revolver.

BADGES OF RANK.

Non-Commissioned Officers.

Infantry, Cavalry, and Artillery.

The distinctive marks are the stripes on the sleeves :—

Corporal—2 worsted chevrons on each cuff.

Sergeant—1 gold or silver chevron on each cuff.

Quartermaster-sergeant—1 gold or silver chevron on each cuff, and 1 stripe of same material above the elbow.

1st sergeant—1 broad and 1 narrow gold or silver chevron on each cuff.

Sergeant-major—2 broad gold or silver chevrons on each cuff.

Squadron, battery, or company sergeant-major (*Premier sergeant-major*, or, in cavalry, *Premier maréchal des logis chef*)—2 broad and 1 narrow gold or silver chevrons on each cuff.

Regimental sergeant-major (*Adjutant sous-officier*)—Officer's forage cap with a horizontal line of gold and silver braid ; epaulettes, half worsted, half gold. In the cavalry and artillery 3 broad gold or silver chevrons on each cuff.

Officers.

Infantry.

The distinctive marks are on the collar, epaulettes, and forage cap.

Those on the two latter are common to all arms.

Rank.	Forage cap. (Number of stripes of lace.)	Epaulettes.	Collar badges.
Sub - lieutenant	2 horizontal, 1 perpendicular (gold).	Silver body, gold edging, gold straight fringe.	1 gold star.
Lieutenant ...	2 horizontal, 2 perpendicular (gold).	Gold body, silver edging, gold straight fringe.	2 gold stars.
2nd captain ...	2 gold horizontal, 2 gold and 1 silver perpendicular.	All gold, straight fringe, a silver cord along the body.	2 gold, 1 silver star.
Captain commandant	2 horizontal, 3 perpendicular (gold).	All gold, straight fringe.	3 gold stars.
Major... ...	3 horizontal, 1 perpendicular (gold).	Silver body, gold edging, gold bullion fringe.	Broad gold lace stripe with 1 silver star.
Lieutenant-colonel	3 horizontal, 2 perpendicular (gold).	Gold body, silver edging, gold bullion fringe.	As above, with 2 silver stars.
Colonel ...	3 horizontal, 3 perpendicular (gold).	All gold, with bullion fringe.	As above, with 3 silver stars.

Artillery.

The distinctive marks on the forage cap and the epaulettes are as for infantry. Artillery officers wear no collar badges. The "lines" vary according to rank, field officers having three tassels with bullion fringe, other officers two tassels with straight fringe. There are other minor differences.

Cavalry.

Forage cap as for infantry.

The distinctive lace on the sleeves is arranged in a pointed knot of narrow stripes of gold or silver lace as follows :—

Sub-lieutentant—One line (gold).

Lieutenant—Two lines (gold).

2nd captain—Three lines (centre one silver).
Captain commandant—Three lines (all gold).
Major—Four lines (all gold).
Lieutenant-colonel—Five lines (centre one silver).
Colonel—Five lines (all gold).

GENERAL OFFICERS.

Rank.	Forage cap.	Epaulettes.	Badges on epaulettes and shoulder cords.
Major-General	4 horizontal, 3 perpendicular stripes, and a round gold cord at bottom of cap.	As for colonels, but with badges.	2 silver stars.
Lieut.-General	As above, with 5 horizontal and 3 perpendicular stripes.		3 silver stars.

CHAPTER X.

SMALL ARMS AND FIELD GUNS AND AMMUNITION.

THE nature of the weapons used by the different [arms has already been indicated. Detailed descriptions of them are given below and in the annexed tables.]

Cavalry sword, light model, 1822 pattern, in steel scabbard : —

Shape ...	...	...	...	Curved.
Length of blade	...		...	36·2 inches.
Weight	...	...	...	2·38 lbs.
Weight with scabbard		...		4·51 lbs.

Old infantry pattern sword, used by dismounted men of artillery : —

Shape...	...	...	...	Slightly curved.
Length of blade	...		...	29·53 inches.
Weight	...	...	...	2·07 lbs.
Weight with scabbard		...		2·53 lbs.

Lance, English pattern, with bamboo staff : —

Length	...	...	...	9·34 feet.
Weight	...	...	...	4·77 lbs.

For descriptions of other small arms, *see* tables, pp. 62 and 63.

SUPPLY OF AMMUNITION IN THE FIELD.*

INFANTRY.

Each infantry soldier carries 30 rounds in time of peace, and 180 rounds on service, distributed as follows :—

On the soldier—

In the pouch	...	...	...	...	60
„ valise	...	...	...	...	60
„ pockets of valise	...	...	...	60

Total	...	...	...	180

In addition 139 rounds per man are carried thus :—

In the company baggage wagon	...	...	12
„ battalion ammunition cart		...	30
„ infantry ammunition column		...	97

Total	...	...	...	139
Grand total	...	...	319	

CAVALRY.

Carbine and Revolver Ammunition.

Carried on the soldier—

	No. of rounds.	
	Peace.	War.
Every man armed with carbine	15	Not known.
„ „ „ revolver	18	—
Total...	33	

---

* Details on this subject are confidential. It has therefore not been possible to verify them officially.

In addition a certain number of rounds per man are carried in the horse artillery ammunition column on service.

———————

At the commencement of an action the infantry soldier is furnished with as many additional rounds (to be carried in the pockets, &c.) as possible, without unduly impeding his movements.

Every favourable opportunity is taken advantage of for filling up, by means of carriers and pack animals, and for replacing expended ammunition in regimental and other reserves. The position of regimental reserves (which should be under cover, and not more than 500 metres in rear of the firing line) and ammunition columns is indicated by day by flags, and by night by lanterns, of distinctive colours. Cartridges of all casualties are collected and reissued. The soldier is trained to use, first, the ammunition which he has in his pockets; secondly, that in the pouch; thirdly, that in the valise.

One packet of ammunition (15 rounds) is always to be left in the pouch, as a last reserve, and is only to be expended by order of the captain of the company.

Cavalry are replenished with ammunition from the nearest infantry ammunition column, or from the horse artillery ammunition column if acting independently. Engineers are supplied from the infantry ammunition columns.

———————

ARTILLERY RESERVE AMMUNITION.

Wagons of artillery ammunition columns are packed in the same manner, and contain the same number of rounds as battery wagons (*see* p. 61).

The total amount of ammunition carried by an ammunition column is therefore as follows :—

	Field artillery ammunition column (14 wagons). Rounds.	Horse artillery ammunition column (5 wagons). Rounds.
Common shell ...	840	360
Shrapnel	420	180
Case	28	10
Total ...	1,288	550

The distribution of the various échelons of a battery in action will be found described in Chapter XVI (3). Unless otherwise ordered the second échelons, as soon as they have taken up their positions, will send three wagons to the first échelons. Ammunition in the limbers is only to be used in case of absolute necessity, and empty ones are to be immediately replaced. Ammunition from the wagons of the first échelon is to be first used ; when empty they are to proceed at a trot to the second échelon to be exchanged for full ones.

Empty wagons of the second échelon are to proceed to the ammunition column to be refilled. In emergencies they may be replaced by full wagons of the ammunition column.

Infantry battalion ammunition wagons when empty are to proceed at a trot to the nearest ammunition column, where they are exchanged for full ones.

	Field 8·7 cm. (3·42 inches).	Horse 7·5 cm. (2·95 inches). Converted to *tir accéléré*, 1904.	Remarks.
Material	Steel	Steel	Guns and wagons are 6-horse.
Breech action	Krupp	Krupp	
Number of grooves	18	16	
Weight of gun	8 cwt. 3 qrs. 12 lbs.	5 cwt. 3 qrs. 17 lbs.	
" " and carriage	22 cwt. 0 qr. 14 lbs.	16 cwt. 3 qrs. 20 lbs.	
" " behind team (with gunner)	50 cwt. 0 qr. 10 lbs.	35 cwt. 1 qr. 20 lbs.	
" " per horse	8 cwt. 1 qr. 10 lbs.	5 cwt. 3 qrs. 17 lbs.	
Number of rounds carried on gun-carriage and limber	34 { 20 common shell / 10 shrapnel / 4 case	40 { 24 common shell / 12 shrapnel / 4 case	
Number of rounds carried on ammunition wagon	92 { 60 common shell / 30 shrapnel / 2 case	110 { 72 common shell / 36 shrapnel / 2 case	
Total number of rounds per battery	1,032 { 660 common shell / 330 shrapnel / 42 case	1,230 { 792 common shell / 396 shrapnel / 42 case	
Number of fuzes carried on gun carriage and limber	37 { 12 time / 25 percussion	43 { 14 time / 29 percussion	
Number of fuzes carried on ammunition wagon	111 { 36 time / 75 percussion	129 { 42 time / 87 percussion	
Total number of fuzes per battery	1,221 { 396 time / 825 percussion	1,419 { 462 time / 957 percussion	
Number of men carried on limber ... ammunition	5	None	
" " wagon	2	2	
Common shell (cast-iron) bursting charge	7 ozs. 6 drs.	3 ozs. 14 drs.	F.G. powder.
Shrapnel " (steel) bursting charge	5 ozs. 2 drs.	1 oz. 15 drs.	
" " number of bullets	165	110	
Case shot	150	100	
Powder charge	3 lbs. 4 ozs.	2 lbs. 3 ozs.	
Muzzle velocity per second	1,168 feet	1,256 feet	
Extreme range of shrapnel	5,140 yards	4,811 yards	

Description of weapon.	Weight of the arm.		Length of the arm.		Barrel.	
	Without bayonet.	With bayonet.	Without bayonet.	With bayonet.	Calibre.	Length.
	lb. oz.	lb. oz.	ft. in.	ft. in.	in.	ft. in.
Rifle—						
Mauser repeating, pattern 1889	8 9	9 6	4 2	5 0	·301	2 6·67
Mauser repeating, pattern 1895	8 13 (nearly)	9 11	4 0	(about) 4 10	·275	2 5·05
Albini, pattern 1867	10 8·2	11 4	4 6·5	6 0·5	·433	2 9·86
Carbine—						
Mauser repeating, pattern 1895	(about) 7 8	(about) 8 6	3 1½	3 11½	·275	1 5·95
Comblain, pattern 1871 ...	6 0·75	—	3 2·5	—	·433	1 10·16
Pistol—						
Browning (for officers) ...	1 6	—	0 6·28	—	·301	0 3·97
Chamelot-Delvigne, 1871 ...	2 4·5	—	0 9·75	—	·433	—
1883 pattern (for N.C.O.'s and men)	—	—	—	—	—	—

* The smokeless powder for the infantry rifle is that known as "L³ Wetteren was adopted by the Belgian Government in 190

N USE IN BELGIAN ARMY.

	Grooves.			Cartridges.						Initial velocity (feet per second).	Remarks.
					Bullet.						
Number.	Width.	Depth.	Twist—one turn in	Weight of charge.*	Weight.	Length.	Total weight.	Total length.			
	in.	in.	ins.	grs.	grs.	ins.	grs.	ins.			
4	·172	·006	9·84	46·29	227·59	1·18	441 36	—		2034·16	Full length of bayonet about 15 ins.
4	·153	·004.	8·66	38·58	172·83	1·21	—	—		2388·49	
4	·169	·012	21·6	77	385	·985	633	2·7		1368	
4	·153	·604	8·66	38·58	172·83	1·21	—	—		2181·80	
4	·169	·012	21·6	77	385	·985	633	2·7		—	
5	—	—	—	3·086	74·04	—	118·31	·98		836	Magazine holds 7 cartridges.
4	·169	·012	—	19	231	·618	309	—		—	
4	—	—	—	15·4	185	—	—	—		—	

user, 1889 pattern," manufactured by the Société Cooppal, at Wetteren. It
er long trials for ballistic and keeping properties.

CHAPTER XI.

ENTRENCHING TOOLS AND CAVALRY PIONEER EQUIPMENT.

INFANTRY.

FIFTY per cent. of the infantry carry the Linneman portable spade, of which the following are the dimensions :—

Total length	19·6 inches.
Length of handle	11·8 ,,
,, blade	7·8 ,,
Breadth of blade	5·9 ,,
Weight ... ... about	26·5 ounces.

For manner of carrying, *see* Chapter III, p. 21.

In addition to the Linneman spade, entrenching tools are carried by the men in the following proportion per company :—

	Peace.	War.
Pickaxes	3	6
Hand-axes	6	12
Saws...	3	3
Billhooks	3	9

Some of these are carried in the company wagon.

CAVALRY PIONEER EQUIPMENT.

This is of two kinds :

(*a*) Ordinary tools for work to be performed by the ordinary trooper.

(*b*) Special tools, with explosives for pioneers.

The following are the ordinary tools carried by a squadron :—

> 8 Linneman spades.
> 4 picks.
> 8 hatchets.
> small tool bags, each containing—
>> 1 pair pincers.
>> 2 gimlets.
>> 1 3-square file.
>> 1 chain-saw with its two handles.
>> 2 cutting and pinching pliers.

The above are always carried on the saddle.
The special tools are as follows :—

> 1 1·3-inch auger, with handle.
> 1 climbing outfit (2 creepers and 1 belt).
> 5 petard bags, each containing—
>> 16 petards.*
>> 2 yards of empty hose canvas,

> 2 artificer's tool-bags, containing—
>> 1 case for 11 Gévelot primers.
>> 5 yards Bickford's fuze.
>> 1 ball of twine.
>> 1 knife.
>> 1 pair crimping pliers.
>> 4 boxes safety matches (will not go out in wind or rain).
>> $\frac{1}{3}$ oz. of tinder.
>> 30 brads.

---

* The petard is a cylindrical cartridge of tonite ($3\frac{1}{8}$ ozs.), fired by a detonator.

CHAPTER XII.

FOOD AND FORAGE AND THEIR SUPPLY IN THE FIELD.

In peace time the daily ration consists of 10½ ozs. of meat and about 1 lb. 10 ozs. of bread. Groceries are paid for under regimental arrangements out of the men's pay.

On service all rations are free. Their composition is fixed by the War Minister on mobilization.

*The following reserve rations are now carried :—

(i) An ordinary reserve ration, consisting of—

Biscuit	...	...	1 lb. 1 oz.
Preserved meat	...	10 ozs.

Compressed ration—

Soup	...	...
Coffee	...	... } 3 ozs.
Salt	...	...

Total weight, 1 lb. 14 ozs.

(ii) An extra reserve ration of soup, coffee, and salt—weight, 3 ozs.

When billeted on the inhabitants in peace time the scale is similar to the above, except that the meat ration is nearly 1 lb., and 2 lbs. of potatoes are supplied.

The full forage ration consists of—

Oats	...	...	...	...	11 lbs.
Hay	...	...	...	...	6½ „
Straw	...	...	...	...	9 „

---

* A ration of about 1½ ozs. of lump sugar will in future be issued to troops at manœuvres, on the line of march or on any continuous duty. It consists of 8 pieces done up in waterproof paper. Part is intended for ordinary sweetening purposes and part to be eaten.

The light ration—

Oats	...	...	...	...	11 lbs.
Hay	...	...	...	...	5½ „
Straw	...	...	...	...	9 „

The reserve ration of oats is 13 lbs. per horse.

The supply of food and forage to the army in the field is dependent on the following sources :—

(1) The inhabitants (when troops are billeted).
(2) Purchase of supplies.
(3) Requisitions.
(4) Depôts established by the Intendance.
(5) Supply columns.
(6) Reserve rations carried regimentally.

The supply of a division is maintained by—

(a) Regimental ration wagons.
(b) *Personnel des subsistences.*
(c) *Équipage d'approvisionnement.*
(d) Supply columns.

Regimental ration wagons carry one day's supply of fresh meat, bread, groceries, and oats necessary for the unit to which they belong. They march with the heavy baggage, join their unit wherever it halts for the night, and, after distributing their loads, go back to the depôts for replenishing.

The depôts are established by the *personnel des subsistences,* and are supplied partly by purchase, partly by the *équipage d'approvisionnement.*

The latter is the medium of replenishment between the depôts and the railway or other locality in connection with the line of communications.

The supply columns carry a reserve supply only to be used when it is impossible to collect supplies from the locality or to obtain them from the base. There are two for each division. The first carries one day's supply of preserved meat, biscuit, groceries, and oats for the division. The second carries the same, without oats.

The reserve ration carried by the troops is issued to them on the outbreak of hostilities. They are not allowed to touch them except by order of the commanding officer, and the greatest care is to be taken of them.

Government establishments exist at Antwerp for baking bread and biscuit, and for making preserved meat rations &c.

CHAPTER XIII.

MARCHES.—ADVANCED AND REAR GUARDS. —BAGGAGE AND TRAINS.

1. RATE OF MARCHING.

Infantry.

THE quick step is at the rate of 120 to the minute, and the length of pace is 29½ inches.

In double time the pace is lengthened to 31·4 inches, and the rate per minute is increased to 165.

The estimated rate of marching is about 2½ miles per hour, including halts, and the average day's march is reckoned at about 22 kilometres (about 14 miles), which is expected to be accomplished in 6 or 7 hours.

Cavalry.

Four paces are laid down :

Walk ... ... 110 metres per minute (or for long marches 100 metres).

Trot ... ... 250 metres per minute (or for long marches 200 metres).

Gallop, ordinary ... 400 metres per minute.

„ accelerated 450 to 500 metres per minute.

Trot and walk ... From 5 to 6½ miles per hour.

(1 metre = 39·37 inches.)

Artillery.

The paces are about the same as for cavalry. The average length of march for artillery alone is 40 kilometres (25 miles), which is usually accomplished on level ground by trotting and walking equally.

With other arms the pace is regulated by that of the infantry.

2. Depth of Marching Columns.

The following are the road spaces occupied by artillery :—

In *column of route* (when not with other troops)-—

Depth of a field battery ... ... 447 yards.
,, horse artillery battery 474 ,,

The distance between each gun and each wagon, &c., in field artillery batteries, is 3 metres (3¼ yards) ; in horse artillery batteries 9 metres (nearly 10 yards).

When marching with other troops, a battery is divided into the following échelons :—

1. *Batterie de combat*... { 6 guns.
4 wagons.
spare horses.

2. *Échelon de ravitaille-ment* ... ... { 5 wagons.
battery cart No. 2.
spare horses.

3. *Échelon de bagages* { battery carts Nos. 1 and 3.
field forge.

The carriages follow one another at 3 metres distance.

In this formation (*marche de guerre*) the depth of batteries is as follows :—

Field Artillevy.

First échelon	...	...	195	yards.
Second ,,	...	...	112½	,,
Interval ...	...	...	21½	,,
			329	,,

Horse Artillery.

First échelon	...	...	171½	yards.
Second ,,	...	...	190	,,
			361½	,,

3. MARCHING FORMATIONS.

Infantry generally marches in columns of fours, cavalry by sections (4 abreast) or half-sections (2 abreast), artillery and other vehicles singly, one following the other.

When approaching the enemy, however, it is considered advisable to diminish the depth of the column, and thus enable it to deploy more rapidly by increasing the front to as great an extent as the road will permit of.

To allow for opening out, the following distances are left in rear of each unit :—

In rear of a company	10	metres
,, squadron, battery, or equivalent unit (ammunition column, &c.)	20	,,
,, battalion, brigade division of artillery, or equivalent unit	30	,,
,, regiment	40	,,
,, brigade	60	,,

4. Halts.

A halt of 10 minutes is made every hour, and takes place simultaneously in every unit of a column after 50 minutes' marching. At the end of the 10 minutes the whole move off again.

If the troops have been concentrated before marching off, and when the march is to exceed 13 to 16 miles, it may be necessary to make a long halt of 1 hour after about two-thirds of the distance have been completed. When the march exceeds 22 miles, or during hot weather, a long halt of 3 to 4 hours may be made in the middle.

Sometimes, in easy country, halts are only made every 2 hours, instead of hourly.

5. Advanced, Rear, and Flank Guards.

The marches of large bodies of troops are covered by the screen of independent or divisional cavalry, as the case may be; but, notwithstanding the protection afforded by these, each unit is covered by its own advanced, rear, and flank guards.

In a column of all three arms, the advanced guard would be composed of from one-sixth to one-third of the infantry, and of the greater portion of the cavalry; artillery, engineer, and other units being added according to circumstances.

The distance from the tail of the advanced guard to the head of the column should not exceed 5,000 metres for a division, nor be less than 500 metres in the case of small detachments.

Advanced guards are divided into three parts— (a) the point, (b) the head, and (c) the main body (gros). In very small bodies (b) is omitted.

The normal formation of an advanced guard of the three arms is briefly as follows:—

The "point" consists of cavalry, varying in numbers

from a few files to a troop, supported at about 300
metres distance by a small body (from a section to a
company) of infantry. Scouts are thrown out to front
and flanks.

The "head" of the advanced guard consists of from
one-fourth to one-third of the infantry, with engineers;
and the main body consists of all the artillery, the
remainder of the infantry, pontoon and telegraph
sections if with the advanced guard, and medical
units.

Rear guards are formed on the same principles.

Flank guards, when required, are told off according
to circumstances. They vary in strength from a few
scouts to companies and sometimes battalions of
infantry, and are always accompanied by cavalry.

In a flank march the column is protected on its
threatened flank by a strong flank guard, of which
the composition is analogous to that of an advanced
guard.

6. Order of March of Main Body.

The commander of the column usually marches at
the head of the largest unit, except in a retreat, when
his place is in rear of it.

The arrangement of the various arms in a column is
such as to enable each to come into action as required.
Artillery is pushed to the front as far as possible, but
is preceded, as a general rule, by at least a battalion of
infantry.

During night marches the infantry is always placed
at the head of the column, and also in narrow valleys
and in long defiles in wooded country, where the exits
on the enemy's side have not been occupied. Artillery
is kept together as much as possible.

7. Baggage and Trains.

The vehicles which follow the troops are divided into 3 categories—

1. First line, or fighting baggage (*train de combat*).
2. Second line, or heavy baggage (*train de bagages*).
3. Train (*convoi*).

In the infantry the regimental transport is thus subdivided—

First line.—Spare horses, ammunition wagons, medical wagon and tool carts. (The above follow the unit to which they belong.)

Second line.—Supply and baggage wagons. (March with second line baggage.)

In the cavalry, spare horses march with their unit; baggage and supply wagons, forage carts, and dismounted men march with second line baggage.

In the artillery, vehicles composing the first échelon (*see* above, p. 70) march with the battery, second échelons in rear of the main body of the column to which their batteries belong. When batteries are attached to cavalry, their first échelons march in rear of the main body of the column to which the batteries belong, the second échelons with the first line baggage. Baggage and supply wagons, and all others not actually required on the field of battle, march with second line baggage.

First line baggage marches in front of the rear guard (in a retreat precedes the advanced guard by some distance) in the following order :—

> Ambulance columns.
> Artillery ammunition columns.
> Infantry   „   „
> Section engineer park.

Second line baggage forms, in the case of divisions and brigades, a separate unit distinct from the column, the rear guard of which it follows at a distance not less than about 1½ miles. It may march by a different road. If necessary, an escort is told off for it.

With units smaller than a brigade, the second line baggage precedes the rear guard. Second line baggage is under the orders of a baggage-master, one being appointed for army headquarters, and one for each division.

The following is usually the order of march :—

Divisional Baggage.

Gendarmerie and prisoners.
Divisional headquarter wagons.
Supply units.
First brigade baggage.
Baggage of non-brigaded units.
Second brigade baggage.
Cattle.

Brigade Baggage.

Brigade staff wagon.
First regiment baggage.
Second regiment baggage.

TRAIN.

The following is the composition of the train (*convoi*) and its order of march :—

Supply wagons.
Field hospitals.
Remount depôt.

The train follows the rear guard at a distance of half a day's march ; it is always quite separate from its column, and may march by a different road. If necessary, a special escort is told off for it.

In a retreat it precedes the second line baggage by half a day's march.

Only the carts and wagons permitted by regulation are allowed to accompany the army, except in cases where special sanction has been obtained. Baggage-masters are directed to turn unauthorised vehicles out of the column, and in case of contumacy to seize the horses.

CHAPTER XIV.

CANTONMENTS, BIVOUACS, AND CAMPS

TROOPS are accommodated either in cantonments (or billets), bivouacs or camps.

Billets are used as often as possible. Bivouacs are, as a rule, only resorted to in case of absolute necessity, and in the immediate neighbourhood of the enemy, but it frequently happens that, in order to avoid breaking up units, troops may be partly in billets and partly in bivouacs around. Camps are only used in special cases, as, for example, during an armistice, or siege.

CANTONMENTS.

The usual manner of quartering troops in the field is in billets or cantonments.

Of these there are two kinds :—

(a) *Ordinary*, used when at a distance from the enemy, or when there is no prospect of an immediate engagement. In this case units may be distributed over large areas with greater comfort to the men.

(b) *Restricted* (*le cantonnement-abri*), *or close quarters*, which are occupied in the vicinity of the enemy, or when other circumstances oblige the troops to be concentrated as much as possible.

In *ordinary cantonments* the troops are generally fed by the inhabitants. The available space is calculated for infantry at the rate of 4 men to a fire—a fire averaging 4 inhabitants—for cavalry at half the above.

In *close quarters*, the object being merely to shelter men and horses from the inclemency of the weather, as many men are crowded in as there is floor-space for, this being calculated at about $2\frac{1}{2}$ yards by 1 yard per man, and $1\frac{1}{2}$ yards by $3\frac{1}{2}$ yards per horse, but there must be free circulation of air.

Units are kept together in one building or group of buildings. The troops prepare their own food.

In all cantonments troops are distributed as far as possible in their order of battle, or order of march, as the case may be, but in order to utilise stabling, cavalry is mixed up with infantry. Artillery, it is laid down, should never be billeted in an isolated position, and its horses must always be near its park.

The quarters of general officers commanding and of staffs are indicated during the day by a flag, and at night by a lantern, of distinctive colours.

BIVOUACS.

As has been stated, bivouacs are only resorted to when circumstances oblige troops to be concentrated and ready for immediate battle, or on the line of march, when the buildings available for sheltering the troops necessitate a too great dispersal of units. The site for a bivouac is selected, as far as possible, out of sight of the enemy, and sheltered from artillery fire, and should be looked for *in rear of*, and sufficiently *close to*, the position to be held, to ensure the latter being occupied before the enemy can seize it. In the case of large bodies of troops prior to an action, units bivouac as much as possible in the relative positions in which they are to fight, and on the line of march they should be echeloned along the road so as to take their places in the column without unnecessary marching. Artillery bivouacs are always protected by infantry.

Troops are bivouacked in one or more lines, or at any rate in several groups sufficiently far apart to facilitate movements, and to avoid units becoming mixed up in case of an alarm. As a rule, a group never consists of less than a regiment.

When corps bivouac one behind the other, the following distances are left, if the ground permits, to allow of freedom of movement and for the latrines, if the latter cannot be placed on one side :—

20 metres between batteries or their equivalents (ammunition columns, &c.).

30 metres between battalions, brigades of artillery,. and similar units.

40 metres between regiments.

60 metres between brigades or different arms of the service.

These spaces may be reduced if necessary, but must never be less than half the above figures.

Latrines should be at least 60 metres from a bivouac.

Infantry Bivouacs.

A battalion bivouacs in double column formation (*see* Chapter XVI), the pelotons being at 15 metres distance. After piling arms, the companies file outwards. The ranks are then opened and the men take off their packs. The fires and cooking places for each peloton are made between the ranks, and in prolongation of the lines of piled arms.

Company officers bivouac 15 metres from the outer flanks and opposite the centre of their company ; battalion staff in rear of the companies. The guard is 20 metres in front of the centre of the battalion.

In normal circumstances a battalion at war strength

occupies, exclusive of latrines, about 158 yards of frontage, by 120 yards of depth.

The battalions of a regiment are placed on one, two, or three lines. The regimental staff bivouacs with the staff of one of the battalions. Only one guard is mounted for the whole regiment, which is always placed in front of the bivouac.

Cavalry Bivouacs.

A cavalry regiment bivouacs in column of squadrons at 87 yards distance between squadrons. In each squadron the front rank moves forward 21 yards. Arms and saddlery are placed, those of the front rank 21 yards in front, and those of the rear rank 21 yards in rear of the lines of horses.

Fires and cooking places are placed on the leeward flank and 21 yards from the horses ; forage a similar distance to windward of them. The officers' fires 21 yards from those of the men. Horses of regimental staff, infirmary and transport, 21 yards in rear of the arms, &c., of the rear squadron. Regimental staff 21 yards in rear of the foregoing. The guard is placed 21 yards in front of the centre of the arms, &c., of the leading squadron.

In normal circumstances a regiment of cavalry of 4 squadrons on war footing occupies, exclusive of latrines, 131 yards of frontage by 393 yards of depth.

Artillery Bivouacs.

The guns and vehicles of a battery are drawn up in 3 lines at a distance of 27 yards apart. The horses are picketed immediately in rear of the vehicles to which they belong ; harness, and the arms of mounted men, are placed 5 yards from the vehicles.

The fires and cooking places for all the men are arranged 82 yards from the first line of vehicles, and the arms and kits of dismounted men 8 yards behind them. The officers' fires, &c., are 15 yards in rear of the men, and the guard 21 yards from the third line of vehicles.

Under normal conditions a battery occupies, exclusive of latrines, 164 yards of front by 185 yards of depth.

A brigade of artillery bivouacs with the batteries either in line or one behind the other. Only one guard is mounted for the division.

CHAPTER XV.

OUTPOSTS.

OUTPOST duties in the Belgian Army, following the usual system, are divided into two parts—" mobile " and "fixed."

The former, consisting in observation, reconnaissance, and the transmission of intelligence, is chiefly confided to the cavalry, although infantry assist by patrols; the latter, in which the main object is resistance, is almost entirely the duty of the infantry.

Where the independent cavalry covers the front of an army the infantry in rear merely occupies with detachments the main approaches and centres of communication. If on the other hand there is no advanced cavalry screen, mixed outposts are formed, cavalry undertaking the mobile, and infantry the fixed, part of the duty.

In close country, or in the proximity of the enemy, when infantry outposts alone are used, cavalry are still attached to the outpost line for the purpose of furnishing advanced posts (*postes d'avis*) and orderlies for the transmission of news.

It is laid down that the occupation of the roads leading towards the enemy is the basis of any system of outposts, and is in most cases quite sufficient to ensure the safety of an army, provided that the intervening ground is well watched by patrols.

Detached posts are used for the protection of exposed flanks, and in dangerous localities.

The complete outpost system provides for the following échelons :—

1. *Le soutien d'avant postes.*
2. *Les grand' gardes.*
3. *Les petits postes avec leurs sentinelles.*
4. *Les postes d'avis.*

These may be roughly described as—

        1. Reserves.
        2. Supports.
        3. Picquets and sentries.
        4. Advanced posts.

In many respects, however, 1 and 2 correspond more nearly to our supports and picquets respectively.

The above system in its entirety is only used for large bodies of troops, or when great vigilance is required. Smaller bodies would only employ 2 and 3, and very small bodies would be content with 3 only, or perhaps would use a few groups of 3 to 6 men under a non-commissioned officer.

Grand' gardes.—These are usually composed of a company, with a certain number of cavalry attached, to furnish orderlies, and in some cases advanced posts.

Each *grand' garde* furnishes one or more *petits postes*, and may also furnish sentries on the group system (3 to 6 men under a non commissioned officer, furnishing a single or double sentry). Reconnoitring patrols are sent out when necessary, and specially a little before nightfall and daybreak. *Grand' gardes* are relieved every 24 hours, usually at daybreak.

Petits postes.—These consist of a peleton, a section, or a squad, under an officer or non-commissioned officer.

They furnish and support the necessary sentries. They are placed from 400 to 600 yards from the *grand' garde.* The sentries are as a rule double. During the day the men not on sentry or patrolling are allowed to sleep. By night all must remain awake. In isolated or exposed positions of importance, groups (*sentinelles renforcées*) are used, furnishing a sentry with relief close at hand. Sentries are relieved either hourly or every 2 hours, and the 2 men forming a double sentry are never relieved together.

Examining guards are placed on the main roads as in our service.

Postes d'avis.—These are generally furnished by the cavalry, and are composed of a non-commissioned officer and a few men, and are pushed forward, according to circumstances, from 2 to 3 miles in front of the *grand' gardes* (or from 1½ to 2 miles if furnished by the infantry).

Their *rôle* is merely that of observation. They post 1 sentry, who is relieved hourly. They are relieved every 6 hours during the day, and not at all by night.

The rules regarding visiting, reconnoitring, and strong patrols, are much the same as in our Army.

CHAPTER XVI.

DRILL AND TACTICS.

1. INFANTRY.

Formations and Movements of a Company.

EACH man is allowed a space of 27 inches in the ranks. The rear rank is placed 1 metre (39 inches) from the front, measuring from heel to heel. Sizing is from right to left, the tallest men being in the rear rank. Changes of front and direction are made by wheeling.

In extended order the normal extension is 1 pace between files, the rear rank man moving up on the left of his front rank man.

Firing is by volleys, independent firing (the number of rounds being stated), independent firing (the number of rounds not being limited), and rapid fire. All loading is, as a rule, through the magazine, which contains 5 cartridges, but the rifle can be used, if necessary, as a single loader.

Front may be diminished by forming fours deep and closing to a flank. The men are also trained to move to a flank by fours or in file.

In the training for battle the soldier is taught that shelter and entrenchments are but secondary considerations, the true force of infantry lying in the intelligent employment of its fire, and in its qualities of brave and stubborn resistance. A soldier is not to avail himself of cover by deviating from the direct line of advance, nor is he to lie down unless ordered to do so.

Signals are used to indicate various movements.

As a rule, independent firing is employed at long and medium ranges, rapid magazine fire being generally reserved until the period immediately preceding the assault. Close formations are to be maintained as long as possible in the attack. After the extension takes place the advance is continued either in quick time or by rushes.

A company consists of 3 pelotons, each of 2 sections. For instructional purposes each peloton consists of not less than 16 files, and each section is numbered from right to left. A company may be formed in column of pelotons at wheeling or quarter distance (about 6 paces). The latter is the formation known as company column. It is, as a rule, formed from line on the centre peloton.

Line of columns of pelotons is formed from line on the right sections, the left sections in rear at 6 paces distance.

In extended order the company is formed, if acting with others, in 2 échelons, viz., firing line and support; if acting alone, in 3, viz., firing line, support, and reserve.

An interval of 6 paces is kept, in the firing line, between each section or peloton.

The normal fighting front of a company is laid down at about 110 yards.

The duties of the various échelons are thus laid down :—

The firing line gains touch with the enemy and opens the action.

The support fills up the gaps in the firing line, gives it ever-increasing intensity of fire, and the necessary forward impulse.

The reserve feeds the advanced échelons, and is available either to make or repel a counter-attack, to pursue, or to cover the retreat.

The distances which should separate the various échelons depend on the nature of the ground and the tactical situation. No precise rules are laid down, the principle being that the action of the firing line must always be adequately sustained.

The formations adopted must be appropriate to the situation, and it is laid down that, as a general rule, the reinforcements should be so regulated that the whole company, practically, should be in the firing line at the distance from the enemy's position from which its fire is most effective, and from which the final assault will be made.

In the defence, great stress is laid on the utility of counter-attacks, and every measure taken should be such as to enable the hottest fire to be brought to bear on the attackers.

Formations and Movements of a Battalion.

The following are the principal formations of a battalion :—

(A) *Line Formations.*

(1) *Line of companies deployed.*—The companies are at 6 paces interval. (For ceremonial use, only used in exceptional cases for manœuvre.)

(2) *Line of company columns.*—The companies may be at any interval not less than 6 paces. (For ceremonial, manœuvre, and combat. It is the formation in which a battalion reassembles after the attack unless orders to the contrary have been given.)

(B) *Column Formations.*

(1) *Double column.*—Formed of 2 columns at 6 paces interval. Each column is composed of 2 company columns, one behind the other at 6 paces distance.

The interval between the columns may be increased

up to half-battalion deploying interval (open double column), and the distance between companies up to the depth of the column at wheeling distance, according to the circumstances and ground. (A manœuvre formation ; occasionally used for ceremonial.)

(2) *Battalion column.*—Corresponding to our quarter column ; companies at 6 paces distance. (For ceremonial ; only occasionally for manœuvre.)

(3) *Open column (à distance entière).*—May be formed of :—

(*a*) Companies in line at a distance equal to their own front plus 6 paces.
(*b*) Companies in column of pelotons.
(*c*)   „   „   sections.
Both the above at wheeling distance plus an additional 6 paces between companies.

(*a*) is a formation for marching past.
(*b*) for marching past, manœuvre, and column of route.
(*c*) for column of route.

With certain exceptions all executive words of command are given by captains.

The battalion sergeant-major (*adjudant sous-officier*) carries a camp colour as a rallying point for the battalion.

Each battalion has a distinctive colour, viz. :—

For all infantry ...	⎰ 1st battalion,		scarlet.
	⎨ 2nd	„	yellow.
	⎱ 3rd	„	black.
For line regiments ...	⎰ 4th	„	scarlet.
Chasseurs and grenadiers	⎱ 5th	„	yellow.
For carabineers... ...	⎧ 4th	„	light green.
	⎪ 5th	„	scarlet.
	⎨ 6th	„	yellow.
	⎩ 7th	„	black.

The flags bear the number or designation of the regiment, and in the case of reserve battalions the letter R.

Great stress is laid on training the men to assemble rapidly and without confusion after being dispersed, and it is laid down that this is to be constantly practised.

Formations of a Regiment.

The following are the fundamental ones laid down :—

(A) *Line Formations.*

(1) *Line,* usually at 30 metres interval between battalions.

(2) *Line of company columns.*—Each battalion in line of company columns at 6 paces, with 30 metres between battalions.

(3) *Line of double columns.*—Each battalion in double column with 30 metres between battalions.

(4) *Line of battalion columns.*—Each in quarter column with 30 metres between battalions.

(B) *Column Formations.*

(1) *Regimental column (colonne de régiment).*—The same as our mass of quarter columns at 30 paces distance.

(2) *Open regimental column (colonne à distance entière).*—The battalions are one behind the other, each in open column, at distances equal to the front of a subdivision plus 30 metres.

The formations and movements of larger bodies are regulated on the foregoing principles, the usual intervals and distances being 40 metres between regiments, 60 metres between brigades, and 80 metres between divisions.

General Principles of Attack and Defence.

Infantry in the presence of the enemy assumes such formations as, without sacrificing mobility, permit of the best use of its fire, while guarding against the effects of that of the enemy.

Concerted action with adjacent bodies and arms of the service is enjoined, and premature extensions are forbidden.

Fire Discipline.

The importance of obtaining a superiority of fire over the enemy is fully recognized.

The duties of the commanders of various units, without being unduly restricted, are generally defined as follows :—

In a battalion the major at the commencement of the fight issues such instructions as the tactical situation demands. He may order the commencement and cessation of fire.

The captains have the task of indicating the object, the distance, and of prescribing the nature of the fire to be used.

Commanders of pelotons and sections see that sights are properly adjusted, and give the words of command.

Great stress is laid on the judicious choice of positions, whether in attack or defence, which admit of obtaining a superiority of fire.

The choice of the objective and of the nature of the fire to be employed depends on the tactical exigencies of the moment.

Volley firing may be used in the attack at long ranges if the conditions are exceptionally favourable, and on the defensive it should be used as long as possible.

Independent firing is, however, regarded as more deadly, but apt to get out of hand.

Long-range firing should be of greater value on

the defensive, where distances ought to be known, than on the offensive, and besides, it frequently causes the enemy to waste ammunition by replying, and to deploy prematurely.

The Battalion in Action.

In the attack the front is not to exceed, as a rule, 300 metres ; in the defence and in making a feint this may be increased.

The fighting formation, whether in attack or defence, comprises a firing line containing 1, 2, or 3 companies which furnish their own supports, and a reserve.

The latter should usually be kept intact until the moment of assault.

If the battalion cannot itself carry the position, this duty will devolve upon the battalions in the second line, which follow in compact formation, gradually closing on the first.

In the defence the general distribution of a battalion is 2 companies in fighting line and 2 in reserve, 1 of which is specially charged with the protection of the flanks.

Tiers of fire are recommended where possible, and opportunities for counter-attacks should be seized whenever they present themselves.

The Regiment in Action.

On approaching the field of action the depth of the column of route is decreased as much as possible.

In the attack the front allotted to a regiment should not exceed 650 yards, but in the defence of a position this may sometimes be increased.

One battalion is usually kept in reserve, or a half battalion if the regiment is acting with others in the defence.

The assault is delivered by the 2nd line, which is

generally formed in 1 or 2 lines of small columns. At the critical moment the 2nd line should not be more the 200 yards from the firing line, followed at a distance of another 200 yards by the third line or reserve.

The Brigade in Action.

The general principles on which a brigade attacks are the same as those laid down for a regiment.

When acting alone it is divided roughly into two parts, the first, including the first and second lines ; the second forming the third line or reserve.

Infantry against Cavalry.

Infantry is taught to rely on its fire to repulse cavalry, and consequently to adopt the formation best adapted to give it full effect.

Groups and squares, therefore, are only formed when there is danger of being enveloped by cavalry, or when surprised.

Infantry and Artillery.

Infantry has the advantage of fire over artillery at ranges under 1,000 metres. Since good observation of the result is so necessary to render artillery fire effective infantry should avoid giving any advantage in this respect.

Localities of which hostile artillery has the range should be avoided or passed at the double.

Infantry should avoid remaining in the immediate neighbourhood of its own batteries as far as possible.

It may be in advance of its own guns, but not nearer than 200 metres when they are firing at ranges of 1,700 metres or more, 300 metres at ranges of 1,400 to 1,700 metres, or 600 metres when firing at 1,200 to 1,400 metres. These distances may, however, be decreased if the supporting artillery occupies a commanding position.

Infantry may be ordered to attack artillery in position, either with a view of capturing it or of creating a diversion.

In the latter case the whole may be extended. In the former it should be divided into two portions, one to attack the battery, the other the support.

Advantage should always be taken of opportunities afforded by the ground, &c., for surprising the enemy, if possible.

Infantry should always be ready to support or protect by its fire batteries in its vicinity.

When artillery is operating at a distance from other arms a special escort is detailed for it. Infantry acting as escort to artillery must be careful not to impede the action of the latter, while at the same time taking every precaution against surprise.

Night Operations.

While recognising the possibility of large bodies of troops having recourse to the cover afforded by darkness for the purpose of making an attack in force, it is laid down that as a rule larger units than battalions will rarely be employed in night operations.

In attacking, except for the purpose of making a feint, firing is not to be employed, the difficulty of directing it with precision rendering it of little use. All attacks must be pressed home with the bayonet.

On the defensive, infantry at night will use volley firing only.

A beaten enemy is not to be pursued.

2. CAVALRY.

Formations and Movements of a Squadron.

The tactical unit of cavalry is the squadron. It consists of 4 troops (occasionally only 3), and is formed in 2 ranks, 1 metre (3·28 feet) between the ranks from head to croup.

Each troop consists of 2 sections, each of from 12 to 18 files.

The files on the right and left flanks of the squadron are left blank. The squadron sergeant-major and quartermaster-sergeant ride there in certain formations.

Each horse is allowed about 1 yard of lateral space. The men ride knee to knee, and are numbered off by fours from the right.

The troop leaders are in front of the centre of their troops—the squadron leaders in front of the right troop of their squadrons. Serrefile rank $1\frac{1}{2}$ metres in rear.

Front may be diminished from troops to sections, half-sections, or single file. Movements to a flank are made by wheeling or the diagonal march.

The usual manœuvring formations of a squadron are, line, line of "troop columns" (troops in fours or file), column of troops (at wheeling distance), and column of route (troops in fours or files following each other).

Rear ranks take an additional *two* yards distance in charging. Cavalry are accustomed to work by signal.

The term "group" has been substituted for that of "division," as applied to the two fractions of a regiment.

Formations of a Regiment.

Line.—Squadrons in line at 12 metres interval.

Line of troop columns.—The squadrons (formed in line of troop columns) are placed on the same alignment at deploying interval.

Line of squadron columns.—The squadrons formed in column of troops are at deploying interval.

Mass.—Line of squadron columns at 12 metres intervals.

Column of troops.—Squadrons, each in column of

troops, one behind the other at such a distance as to preserve their interval if wheeled into line.

Column of route.—Squadrons formed in column of route following each other at 25 metres distance.

Distances and intervals may always be modified if necessary.

Flanking squadrons are placed in échelon on the flank at a distance equal to their front plus 12 metres, and are formed in column of troops.

The strength of a reserve is laid down as from one-third to one-fourth of the whole force ; its duties are to be ready for the unexpected ; in case of success to complete the route of the enemy, and in case of repulse to cover the retirement of the main body by a counter-attack. Its position is no longer defined.

General Principles.

Prompt appreciation of the tactical situation, rapidity of decision, and boldness verging on rashness are the qualities to be aimed at by a good cavalry commander.

Cavalry manœuvres in column, and attacks in line or extended order. Its *rôle* is essentially offensive.

Formations are classified as those for *march, assembly, approach, manœuvre,* and *attack.*

Column of troops is recommended as an intermediate formation between those for marching and assembly. Its front is small, it is handy and forms line rapidly to a flank, but when used for large bodies its deployment to the front is less rapid than that of other columns.

Assembly formations are *mass* for group or regiments *line* or *column* of masses for larger units.

Mass takes up the least space while retaining mobility.

Line of squadron columns is very flexible, and suitable to any ground. It admits of the most rapid deployment, and gives less mark for artillery than mass. It is the most suitable formation preparatory to attacking.

Marches of approach are executed according to the ground in a massed formation or in several columns of troops when likely to be exposed to artillery fire.

Manœuvre formations are usually lines of squadron or troop columns.

Line of troop columns is also a very supple and handy formation which adapts itself very rapidly to accidents of the ground.

Line is essentially the fighting formation, but should be avoided for manœuvring.

Extended order is for employment against artillery and infantry skirmishers, also in the pursuit. It should not be used in too large bodies on account of the difficulty of rallying.

Formations in single rank are used when opposed to cavalry to impose upon the enemy by the display of apparently superior force.

Combat patrols, officer's patrols, and ground scouts are used. In the former it is calculated that in ordinary country 30 men can cover a front of 2,500 yards.

Dismounted action.—It is recognised that dismounted fire-action adds greatly to the usefulness of cavalry, which uses the rifle either when it cannot use the "arme blanche," or when it can attain its object better by fire than by shock action. For dismounted work the squadron or other commander tells off such part or parts of his command as he considers necessary, the remainder forming the "mounted reserve." Troop-leaders tell off horse-holders from among the worst shots or men who have no carbines. Two per troop is considered sufficient.

Cavalry is recommended to profit by its great mobility, and to use fire-action for surprises or ambuscades. The mounted reserve is intended to watch the flanks and rear of the dismounted men, and to protect the led horses, to pursue, or to cover the retirement of the skirmishers.

Formations and Movements of a Brigade.

The following are the formations of a cavalry brigade :—

> Line.
> Line of columns.
> Line of masses.
> Column of masses.
> Column of troops.

In *line*, regiments are deployed at 12 metres interval.

Column of route (25 metres between regiments).

In *line of columns*, regiments formed in line of squadron columns are at squadron deploying interval, plus 12 metres.

In *line of masses*, regiments in mass are at squadron deploying interval, plus 12 metres ; in column formations 25 metres distance are kept between regiments.

In *column of masses*, the regiments, in mass, are formed one behind the other at a distance of 24 metres.

In *column of troops* 24 yards distance is kept between regiments.

Distances and intervals may be modified according to ground and circumstances.

Cavalry against Infantry.

It is laid down that the attack of unbroken infantry is only to be carried out in critical or decisive circumstances, such as to stop, at all hazards, the victorious advance of an enemy when no fresh infantry is available. Cavalry being an arm difficult to renew in the course of a campaign, the sacrifices demanded of it

(8674)   H

should be in proportion to the advantage it is expected to gain. As a rule, infantry can only be successfully attacked by cavalry when in disorder or demoralized, or at other times when surprised. A screen of men attacking in extended order is recommended to mask the real attack.

3. ARTILLERY.

Field and Horse.

The tactical unit of artillery is the brigade (*see* Chapter V); the unit of fire is the battery. The battery is divided into 4 sections, the first 3 containing each 2 guns and 3 wagons, the fourth the remainder of the wagons, &c.

Formations.

Line (for reviews). — Full interval 13 metres (14·2 yards) for field artillery ; 19 metres (20 yards) for horse artillery. This interval may be increased or diminished. Mounted detachments are 5 metres in rear of their guns.

The front of a gun is reckoned at 2 metres.

The front of a mounted detachment at 4 metres.

The depth of a mounted detachment at 5 metres.

In action.—Full interval as in line. Reduced ntervals are only used where space is limited.

A battery in action is usually disposed as follows :—

1st line—6 guns.

2nd line—2 ammunition wagons in rear of Nos. 2 and 5 guns.

3rd line (in rear and to a flank of the battery, as far as 200 yards if necessary)—6 limbers ; 2 wagons (ammunition) ; spare horses.

The above form the first échelon.

4th line (in any position about 800 metres in rear having good communications to front and rear)—

5 wagons (ammunition) ; 1 wagon (G.S.) ; spare horses.

Forming the second échelon (*échelon de ravitaillement*).

Column.—

(*a*) Of sections (2 guns) at full or reduced interval.
(*b*) Of subdivisions at 2 yards distance.

Artillery in Action.

The value of artillery lies in its fire, and in the moral support which it gives to other troops. Its effectiveness is dependent on the accuracy with which the observation of its fire can be carried out, and its employment is therefore limited by the range of vision.

Common shell is not considered effective against troops beyond 2,900 metres, unless it can be very exactly regulated. It is used for ranging.

Shrapnel produces its greatest effect when the distance of its burst, in front of the object aimed at, is between 50 and 100 yards, although at medium ranges it will be sufficiently effective if it bursts at the normal height up to 150 yards in front of the object.

Fire is divided into—(1) ordinary ; (2) slow ; and (3) rapid.

In (1) the interval between each shot is from 15 to 20 seconds ; (2) is used at long ranges when there is a deficiency of ammunition or when observation is difficult ; the interval between rounds varies ; (3) is used up to 1,900 metres in cases where it is desired to take immediate advantage of a favourable opportunity.

Concentration of fire is enjoined, and changes of position are to be avoided as far as possible.

Artillery commences most battles at ranges depending on the nature of the ground. In favourable

(8674)   H 2

country the positions will usually be sought for at about 3,000 metres from the enemy. The first target will be the opposing artillery. When this has been silenced the artillery will turn its attention to preparing the way for the attack of its own infantry, and it may be necessary for this object to take up a second position nearer the point of attack.

At this precise period all the energies of the artillery must be directed towards supporting the infantry, even to the extent of somewhat exposing itself, in order to contribute towards the support of the troops destined for the assault.

If the position is carried, part of the batteries without delay advance to complete the success and assist in the pursuit, the remainder direct their fire against the enemy's reserves, and against any troops which may attempt to rally or to retake the offensive.

If the assault fails, all the batteries concentrate their fire on the defending troops to prevent their taking the offensive, and to allow the attacking infantry to reform.

On the defensive, fire is frequently opened at long ranges by a certain number of batteries pushed in front of or outside the limits of the position, and protected by cavalry or by advanced parties of the defenders. The object is to deceive the enemy as to the real position occupied, and to cause premature deployments which may disclose his designs, and above all to prevent his artillery from seizing at the outset favourable positions for attack.

As soon as these objects are attained, and the batteries detailed for them find themselves exposed to superior fire, they fall back on the main position.

When all uncertainty as to the point of attack has ceased, artillery, in order to obtain a superiority, should put every gun in action, the essential point being (while endeavouring to keep down the fire of the hostile artillery) to weaken and check the assaulting infantry.

In case of defeat, the artillery retires by successive échelons, giving mutual support to one another and to the retreating troops.

It is on such occasions that artillery should in case of necessity sacrifice itself to save a disaster.

Employment of Horse Artillery with Cavalry Division.

Artillery acting with cavalry should be kept intact, the better to regulate the effectiveness of its fire, and to avoid multiplying lines of fire which might interfere with cavalry action.

In marches prior to an action one battery is kept with the advanced guard. The remainder marches with the column formed by the first line.

When the cavalry division assumes its preparatory fighting formation the artillery, formed in mass, is generally placed in advance of the front, or of one of the flanks. The escort scouts for and protects the batteries ; occasionally when the ground is such as to render a surprise possible, the artillery takes up a position in rear of the cavalry.

During the action the artillery should not be tied as regards its position to the cavalry, but it should on the contrary aim at establishing itself in the most favourable position to support the cavalry by its fire, without impeding the movements of the latter. It should open fire as quickly as possible to support the deployment, and should continue it during the charge, first on the enemy's artillery and first lines, afterwards on the reserves and again on the batteries.

One half squadron is attached to it as escort, to act as ground scouts and to brush away small hostile bodies. It is incumbent, however, on the nearest large body to come to the assistance of the artillery should it be necessary.

APPENDIX I.—DISTRIBUTION OF ACTIVE ARMY.

TABLE A.

INFANTRY.

Corps.	Peace Station.	Unit of Field Army to which it belongs and Peace Headquarters of that Unit.
1st regiment of the line	Ghent	1st brigade (Ghent) ⎤
2nd ,,	Ghent and Termonde	} I Division (Ghent).
3rd ,,	Ostend and Ypres	2nd brigade (Bruges) ⎦
4th ,,	Bruges	
5th ,,	Antwerp	3rd brigade (Antwerp) ⎤
6th ,,	,,	} II Division (Antwerp).
7th ,,	,,	4th brigade (Antwerp) ⎦
8th ,,	Brussels	
9th ,,	Arlon, Louvain, and Antwerp	5th brigade (Brussels) ⎤
10th ,,		} III Division (Liége).
11th ,,	Haselt and Vilvorde	6th brigade (Liége) ⎦
12th ,,	Liége and Verviers	
13th ,,	Namur	9th brigade (Namur)—(fortress troops, mobile).
14th ,,	Liége	
1st chasseurs à-pied	Charleroi and Diest	7th brigade (Mons) ⎤
2nd ,, ,,	Mons	} IV Division (Brussels).
3rd ,, ,,	Tournai and Antwerp	8th brigade (Brussels) ⎦
Grenadier regiment	Brussels	
Carabineer ,,	,,	1 battalion to each division.

TABLE B.

CAVALRY.

Corps.	Peace Station.	Unit of Field Army to which assigned and Peace Headquarters of that Unit.	
1st Guides	Brussels	...	1st brigade (Brussels) } 1 Cavalry Division (Brussels).
2nd ,, ...	,, ...	...	
1st Lancers	Namur	...	2nd brigade (Namur)
2nd ,, ...	Liége	...	
1st Chasseurs-à-cheval...	Tournai	...	3rd brigade (Mons) } II Cavalry Division (Ghent).
2nd ,, ...	Mons	...	
3rd Lancers	Bruges	...	4th brigade (Ghent)
4th ,, ...	Ghent and Oudenarde ...	...	

TABLE C.

ARTILLERY.

Regiment.	Peace Station.	Unit of Field Army to which assigned on mobilization.	Remarks.
	FIELD AND HORSE ARTILLERY.		
1st regiment	Ghent and Antwerp	1st division.	2 H.A. batteries at Malines.
2nd ,, ,, ...	Malines, Antwerp, and Tirlemont	2nd division and 2nd cavalry division.	
3rd ,, ,, ...	Brussels and Tirlemont... ...	4th division.	
4th ,, ,, ...	Louvain	3rd division and 1st cavalry division.	
	FORTRESS ARTILLERY.		
Antwerp Position Artillery (1st, 2nd, 3rd, 4th, 5th, 6th, 7th, 8th battalions, plus 3 batteries at Termonde)	Antwerp, Termonde, Diest, Lierre, and all detached forts	} Fortress defences ..	Special companies at Antwerp, part of the armourers at Liége.
Liége Position Artillery (1st, 2nd, 3rd, and 4th battalions)	Liége and detached forts in vicinity		
Namur Position Artillery (1st, 2nd, and 3rd battalions)	Namur, Huy, and detached forts		

TABLE C—*continued.*

ENGINEERS.

Regiment.	Peace Station.	Unit of Field Army to which assigned on mobilization.	Remarks.
1st battalion	Antwerp... ...	1 company to each division.	
2nd ,, ...	,, ...	Antwerp defences.	
3rd ,, ...	Liége ...	Defences of Liége.	
4th ,, ...	Namur ...	,, Namur.	
5th ,, ...	Antwerp... ...	Antwerp defences.	
6th ,, ...	,, ...	,, ,,	
	SPECIAL	COMPANIES.	
Field telegraph ...	Antwerp... ...	With field army and fortress troops.	
Submarine mining, &c. ...	,, ...	Antwerp.	
Railway...	,, ...	With army headquarters.	
Pontoon	,, ...	With field army and fortress troops.	
Labourers and balloon section. ...	,, ...	,, ,,	

TABLE D.

FIELD ARMY.

I. Division.	Station.	II. Division.	Station.
Headquarters	Ghent.	Headquarters	Antwerp.
1st brigade { 1st regiment of the line	,,	3rd brigade { 5th regiment of the line	,,
(Ghent) { 2nd ,, ,,		(Antwerp) { 6th ,, ,,	,,
2nd brigade { 3rd ,, ,,	Ostend.	4th brigade { 7th ,, ,,	,,
(Bruges) { 4th ,, ,,	Bruges.	(Antwerp) { 8th ,, ,,	
1st battalion carabineer regiment	Brussels.	2nd battalion carabineer regiment	Brussels.
1st company engineers	Antwerp.	2nd company engineers	Antwerp.
1st regiment artillery (8 field batteries)	Ghent.	2nd regiment artillery (7 field batteries)	Malines.
1 squadron gendarmerie	Bruges.	1 squadron gendarmerie	Tournai.
1 ,, ,,	Ghent.	1 ,, ,,	Mons.
1st company train	Antwerp.	2nd company train	Antwerp.
1st company battalion of administration	Ghent.	2nd company battalion of administration	
A section field telegraph	Antwerp.	A section field telegraph	Malines.
Detachment of administration	Ghent.	Detachment of administration	Antwerp.
2 artillery ammunition columns	Termonde.	2 artillery ammunition columns	,,
2 infantry ammunition columns	Antwerp.	2 infantry ammunition columns	Antwerp.
1 section engineer park	Termonde.	1 section engineer park	,,
"Equipage d'approvisionnement"	,,	"Equipage d'approvisionnement"	Brussels.
Ambulance column	,,	Ambulance column	Antwerp.
Supply column	,,	Supply column	Malines.
Remount depôt.*	,,	Remount depôt.*	
2 field hospitals	,,	2 field hospitals	Antwerp.

* Non-existent in peace-time.

TABLE D.—*continued.*

FIELD ARMY.

III. Division.	Station.	IV. Division.	Station.
Headquarters ...	Liège.	Headquarters ...	Brussels.
5th brigade { 9th regiment of the line ...	Brussels.	7th brigade { 1st chasseurs-à-pied	Charleroi.
(Brussels) 10th ,, ,,	Arlon.	(Mons) { 2nd ,, ,,	Mons.
6th brigade { 11th ,, ,,	Hasselt.	8th brigade { 3rd ,, ,,	Tournai.
(Liège) 12th ,, ,,	Liège.	(Brussels) { grenadier regiment	Brussels.
3rd battalion carabineer regiment ...	Brussels.	4th battalion carabineer regiment ...	Antwerp.
3rd company engineers ...	Antwerp.	4th company engineers ...	Brussels.
4th regiment artillery (7 field batteries)	Louvain.	3rd regiment artillery (8 field batteries)	
1 squadron gendarmerie...	Namur.	1 squadron gendarmerie ...	Camp, Beverloo.
1 ,, ,,	St. Troud.	1 ,, ,,	Brussels.
3rd company train ...	Antwerp.	4th company train ...	Antwerp.
3rd company battalion of administration	Liège.	4th company battalion of administration	Brussels.
A section field telegraph ...	Antwerp.	A section field telegraph ...	Antwerp.
Detachment of administration ...	Lierre.	Detachment of administration ...	Brussels.
2 artillery ammunition columns ...	,,	2 artillery ammunition columns ...	,,
2 infantry ammunition columns ...	,,	2 infantry ammunition columns ...	,,
1 section engineer park ...	Antwerp.	1 section engineer park... ...	Antwerp.
" Equipage d'approvisionnement " ...	Lierre.	" Equipage d'approvisionnement " ...	Brussels.
Ambulance column ...	,,	Ambulance column ...	,,
Supply column ...	,,	Supply column ...	,,
Remount depôt.* ...	,,	Remount depôt.* ...	,,
2 field hospitals ...	,,	2 field hospitals ...	,,

* Non-existent in peace-time.

CAVALRY.

I. Division.	Station.	II. Division.	Station.
Staff	Brussels.	Staff	Ghent.
1st brigade { 1st guides ...	"	3rd brigade { 1st chasseurs à cheval...	Tournai.
(Brussels) 2nd ,, ...	,,	(Mons) 2nd ,,	Mons.
2nd brigade { 1st lancers...	Namur.	4th brigade { 3rd lancers ,,	Bruges.
(Namur) 2nd ,, ...	Liége.	(Ghent) 4th ,, ...	Ghent.
38th horse artillery battery	Louvain.	18th horse artillery battery ...	Malines.
39th ,, ,, ...	,,	19th ,, ,, ...	,,
1st section of 6th company train ...	Antwerp.	2nd section of 6th company train ...	Antwerp.
Detachment of administration (from 3rd company)	Liége.	Detachment of administration (from 1st company)	Ghent.
Artillery ammunition column...	Lierre.	Artillery ammunition column ...	Malines.
Ambulance column	Brussels.	Ambulance column	,,

N.B.—First five squadrons of each cavalry regiment go with headquarters.
6th squadron ... ... Mobile fortress troops.

APPENDIX II.

HISTORICAL NOTE.

The Kingdom of Belgium formed itself into an independent State in 1830, having previously been part of the Netherlands. The secession was decreed on October 4th, 1830, by a Provisional Government established in consequence of a revolution which broke out at Brussels on August 25th, 1830. A national congress elected Prince Leopold of Saxe-Coburg King of the Belgians on June 4th, 1831; the Prince accepted the dignity July 12th, and ascended the throne July 21st, 1831. By the Treaty of London, November 15th, 1831, the neutrality of Belgium was guaranteed by Austria, Russia, Great Britain, and Prussia. It was not until after the signing of the Treaty of London, April 19th, 1839, which established peace between King Leopold I and the Sovereign of the Netherlands, that all the States of Europe recognised the Kingdom of Belgium.

By Article VII of the above treaty it was agreed that Belgium should form an independent and perpetually neutral State, and should be bound to observe such neutrality towards all other States.

APPENDIX III.

MONEY, WEIGHTS, AND MEASURES.

The Franc ... Par value 25.22½ to £ sterling.
Belgium was one of the five Continental States—comprising, besides, Frace, Italy, Greece, and Switzerland—which formed a Monetary League in 1865.

The Kilogramme ...	2·20 lbs. avoirdupois.
„ Tonne	2·200 lbs. avoirdupois.
„ Hectolitre (dry measure) ...	2·75 Imperial bushels.
„ Hectolitre (liquid measure) ...	22 Imperial gallons.
„ Metre	3·28 feet.
„ Metre Cube ...	35·31 cubic feet.
„ Kilometre ...	1,093 yards.
„ Hectare	2·47 English acres.
„ Square Kilometre	247·11 English acres, or 0·386 square mile.

APPENDIX IV.

PART I.—WAR OFFICE ORGANISATION.

GENERAL REMARKS.

Belgium is a constitutional Monarchy. Legislation is vested in two Chambers—namely, the Senate and the Chamber of Deputies.

The King commands* the land and sea forces, declares war, and makes treaties of peace, alliance and commerce, informing the Chambers of these treaties when the interest and safety of the State permit.

Under him the War Minister, who as a rule is a general officer, is responsible for the efficiency and general administration of the Army. He is a member of the Cabinet, and has a seat in both Chambers, without election, but does not vote or take part in strictly political debates.

He may† delegate part of the duties entrusted to him under such conditions and within such limits as he may determine, to the officials of his department.

Table I‡ shows the War Office organisation, together with the general scope of the duties of each branch, which are given in detail in the Belgian Army List.

Table II‡ shows in similar fashion the relations of the War Office with the high commands and services of the Army.

---

* Belgian Constitution, Art. 68.
† Royal Order of May 15, 1878, No. 4957.
‡ *See* Tables at end.

Numbers and Employments of Officers and Civilians.

At present there are 80 officers and 116 civilian clerks employed* in the offices of the War Ministry.

The first 5 general directions are held by officers, and the 6th by an intendant-general ; of the 6 directions, 3 are held by officers, 1 by an intendant, and 2 by civilians ; of the 29 bureaus, or offices, only 7 are held by civil clerks, namely, those dealing with the secretariat or chancery, foreign armies, militia, substitution, accounts, civil *personnel*, and War Office material ; 5 are held by sub-intendants, and the remaining 17 by officers, the chief posts being occupied by officers who have passed through the Staff College.

System of Work at the War Office. Relations of the Ministers and the Directors-General.

In all matters of daily routine the Minister works directly with the general directions.

The latter lay before him, either verbally or in writing, all matters requiring his decision.

The Minister usually signs all important despatches and memoranda, but leaves purely routine transactions to be dealt with by the Directors-General.

Finance.

The disposal of funds is delegated by the Minister to the Directors-General, each of whom administers his own share.

There is a chapter in the estimates for unforeseen expenses, which is administered by the 6th general direction, and only issued with the approval of the Minister.

---

* *See* Table III.

All papers on financial matters which have to be approved by the Minister, or by the chief intendant, have to be marked as seen and verified by the chiefs of directions.

Indents for pay, seen and verified by directors, are handed to the 3rd bureau, 6th direction, and the latter transmits them to the court of accounts to be liquidated.

When they return, after liquidation, and after having been seen by the Finance Department, the same bureau makes a list of them, according to the chapter and article of the budget they refer to, and exchanges them for a receipt with the chiefs of directions who have issued them ; the directors-general then send the orders for payment to the parties concerned through the competent authorities.

PART II.—SYSTEM OF COMMAND, INSPECTION AND DECENTRALISATION.

I.—GENERALS COMMANDING DISTRICTS (1).*

Generals commanding districts are under the direct orders of the War Minister. A division of the field army is assigned to each district, whose chief commands the corresponding division.

Generals commanding districts have complete authority at all times, over the infantry and field artillery units under their command, in all matters of discipline ; and territorial authority over all other troops in the district. They are responsible for the entire training of the infantry and for the tactical instruction of the field artillery of their division.

At other times than at manœuvres, whenever they intend to have drills or exercises, where all arms are

---

* The figures in *italics* refer to Table II at end.

(8674)   I

represented, they warn the *commandant supérieur* of cavalry (see p. 117), the inspectors-general, and the chief intendant. In case troops have to be called upon to keep order this step may be omitted.

They inspect all units of infantry and field artillery in barracks, camps, or polygons, accompanied by their chief of the staff, and each year they visit the mobilisation centre of their division, accompanied by all the heads of the various services, and take steps to ascertain that all measures have been taken in view of mobilising with the least possible delay.

The intendants and doctors of the division are directly under the general commanding the district, but without prejudice to the special duties of the Chief Intendant and Inspector-General of the Medical Service, whose *rôle* will be referred to presently.

The divisional intendants superintend the administrative services which are under them, and keep the district commander informed of the situation of all the branches of administration.

II.—Governors of Fortified Positions.

These officers have to take all steps necessary for improving the defences of the positions entrusted to them, and prepare all measures which have to be taken in a state of war or siege.

In those positions where no military governor exists in peace time, the president of the local defence committee has the same duties.

The governors act as commandants of infantry and fortress artillery troops told off for the defence of the position, without prejudice to the territorial authority of the district commander and the *rôle* of the inspector-general of artillery.

This duty of a governor does not extend over the reserve battalions of regiments in the infantry division, nor over reserve field batteries.

The authority of the governors is exercised through the infantry brigade commander so far as relates to the infantry arm.

The governors preside at the meetings of the defence committees which keep the defence scheme and plan of mobilisation of the fortress up to date.

III.—INSPECTOR-GENERAL OF ARTILLERY (*3*).

This officer is under the orders of the War Minister, and directs the technical instruction of the whole of the *personnel* of the artillery.

He has command of all artillery troops which are not under the orders of the district commanders or military governors of fortresses ; he also commands the *personnel* of the train regiment.

He makes any proposals he thinks fit regarding technical instruction, but when these changes involve tactical modifications he has to consult with district commanders and governors of fortresses.

He lays before the War Minister, for his approval, his proposals for artillery practices, and his programme for the school of gunnery, as well as all schemes for courses to be followed by officers and others in artillery arsenals and manufacturing establishments.

He proposes any changes of garrison, of artillery units, or officers, in collaboration with the district commanders or governors of fortresses concerned, and makes proposals for any special employment for artillery *personnel*.

He inspects all artillery units in their technical efficiency, reports results to the War Minister, and exchanges confidential reports with district commanders and governors of fortresses.

He presides over the artillery committee, and sits on the fortress and staff committees, and the *conseil de perfectionnement* (see p. 120) of military instruction.

Officers Commanding Artillery in the Army Divisions.

These officers are under the district commanders as regards *personnel*, tactical instruction and mobilisation of field batteries, reserve batteries, and eventually of divisional horse artillery.

They are responsible to the inspector-general of artillery as regards technical instruction of the same units.

Officers Commanding Artillery in Fortified Positions.

These officers are in charge of the fortress artillery *personnel* and material in their commands.

They come under the War Ministry as regards material, under the inspector-general of artillery as regards technical instruction, and under the governor of the fortress in all other matters.

They superintend arsenals, arms, ammunition, buildings, and all material relating to artillery in their command ; sit on the defence committee, and supply the governor with all information required.

Chief Intendant (7).

The military intendant is the director-general of administration at the War Department.

He arranges the estimates for units of troops in the army each year, superintends and checks the accounts of all corps and services generally, except those of the artillery and engineer material.

He is responsible for the financial and technical wellbeing of the establishments of administration.

After seeing the reports of the district commanders and governors of fortresses as regards the requirements of their commands, he submits proposals for the yearly grant of funds to carry out work sanctioned, and he himself initiates and carries out all schemes approved by the Minister for creating depôts of supplies and provisions to meet the requirements of the army both in peace and war.

In all that concerns the *personnel* of his services he acts as commanding officer, making proposals for nominations, promotions, and exchanges among the intendance officials, pay officers, and officers of administration.

The Commandant Supérieur of Cavalry (2).

The cavalry is placed under a general officer with the above title.

He possesses, as regards his branch, the same rights and privileges as are conferred by the regulations upon generals commanding divisions.

He has under his orders the generals commanding cavalry divisions, with whom he corresponds upon all matters relating to the regulations and the service of the arm.

He gives his advice on all proposals submitted to the Minister, and presides over the committee of generals inspectors of the cavalry.

He may inspect regiments whenever he pleases.

Except in so far as affected by the above, the officers commanding cavalry divisions have all powers and duties confided to them by the regulations.

Inspector-General of Engineers (4).

The Inspector-General of Fortifications and of the Corps of Engineers is under the direct orders of the Minister of War.

He superintends all fortresses, forts, lines, establishments, and military buildings, making proposals for their alteration, care, or sale, as the case may be.

(8674)   I 2

as well as for the construction of new defences and the maintenance of old ones.

Before inspecting fortifications he has to receive orders from the War Minister. He advises the latter on all matters connected with fortifications and buildings, and makes such suggestions as the interest of the State requires.

CHIEF OF THE STAFF CORPS (8) AND STAFF COMMITTEE.

The Chief of the Staff Corps is under the direct orders of the Minister of War.

He takes part, under the direction of the Minister, in the examination of all fundamental questions relating to the organisation and mobilization of the army and the study of plans of operations.

He sits on the *conseil de perfectionnement* of the establishment for military instruction.

He lays before the staff committee all matters upon which its opinion is required, and lays the result before the War Minister.

He initiates all measures calculated to improve the service of the staff, or to develop the theoretical and practical knowledge of its officers, and makes all proposals for the promotion and employment of officers of the staff corps, with the advice and assistance of the staff committee. All reports and notes of confidential reports on staff officers are kept by him.

He receives each year from the Inspectors-General a copy of the remarks upon staff officers whose work has come under their observation, and he sends to the inspectors his own notes upon the *adjoints d'état major* who are employed on the staff or attached to other arms.

All instructions concerning staff work emanate from him ; he inspects the staff *personnel* and reports on the same to the Minister, sending extracts to generals commanding districts.

He also transmits to the Minister, with his remarks, special papers, reports, or *mémoires* prepared under his orders by staff officers.

The Staff Committee is composed of :—

The General Officer, Chief of the Staff Corps.
A general officer of Infantry.
A general officer of Cavalry.
The Inspector-General of Artillery.
The Inspector-General of Engineers.
A general officer or colonel from the *cadre spécial* of the staff.

All proposals concerning the staff are laid before this Committee by the Chief of the Staff Corps ; it examines and discusses all questions relating to the composition and organisation of the staff *personnel* appreciates the merits of the work done by officers and classifies the latter in a list forwarded to the War Minister by December 1st of each year.

After taking note of the remarks of the Inspector-General, the Committee makes its proposals for the admission, ordinary or exceptional promotion, re-integration in their regiments, non-employment or retirement of officers of the staff.

The Committee meets at times fixed by the War Minister, and also whenever the necessity arises, is assembled by the Chief of the Staff Corps in the name of the Minister of War.

The presidency of the Committee is taken by the senior member, the staff officer of the Chief of the Staff Corps acting as secretary.

The deliberations of this body are secret ; the proceedings of the meeting, signed by all the members present, are sent to the War Minister.

INSPECTOR-GENERAL OF THE MEDICAL SERVICE (5).

This Inspector is under the direct orders of the Minister of War.

All medical officers are under his supervision in all matters relating to their service.

Chiefs of the Medical Service in garrisons inform him of all demands for leave and of all changes of *personnel* under their orders. They also keep him informed of any changes in the *état-civil* of the *personnel*, and of all honorary distinctions obtained.

All applications made to their military superiors by medical officers have to be first submitted for the advice of the Inspector General.

CHIEF VETERINARY OFFICER (6).

This officer corresponds directly with the War Minister and with commanders of units.

He has to reply to all military officers who ask for his opinion. He maintains touch with the veterinary chiefs of services so as to keep himself informed of the condition of horses in the army.

CONSEIL DE PERFECTIONNEMENT.

This Council has been created to supervise and improve the educational establishments in the army.

It may consist of 10 members, but must include the following :—

A general officer of the Staff Corps.
         „   „   Infantry.
         „   „   Cavalry.
         ,   „   Artillery.
         „   „   Engineers.
The Commandant of the Staff College.
         „   „   „   Military School.

The second in command at the Staff College acts as secretary, and keeps the archives of the Council.

Its members are nominated by Royal Order, but they may not include professors at any military instructional establishment ; the senior officer presides.

It advises the Minister as to the nominations to professorships proposed by the commandants of the Staff College and Military School.

It gives the Minister an opinion upon the programme framed by a newly-appointed professor ; the members may attend the lectures at the Staff College and Military School, and make any suggestions as to changes in the general plan of studies or special courses.

The Council act as examiners of officers passing out of the Staff College, and one of their members presides at the examinations at the end of the first and second year.

The Council always meets from October 1st to 15th, when it receives reports on educational establishments sent to the War Office by the various generals and heads of educational schools and colleges, and makes a general report to the Minister on the subject.

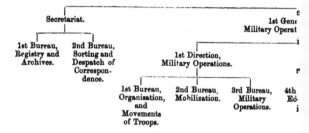

Secretariat.

1st Bureau,
Registry and
Archives.

2nd Bureau,
Sorting and
Despatch of
Correspon-
dence.

1st Direction,
Military Operations.

1st Bureau,
Organisation,
and
Movements
of Troops.

2nd Bureau,
Mobilization.

3rd Bureau,
Military
Operations.

4th
Ed

e
1st Gene
Military Operat

(8674)

TABLE I.

War Office Organisation, Belgium.

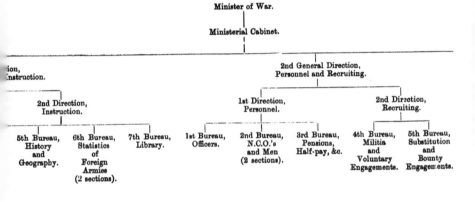

Minister of War.

Ministerial Cabinet.

| ...ion, Instruction. | | | 2nd General Direction, Personnel and Recruiting. | | | | |

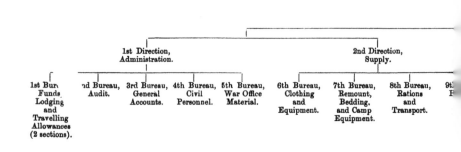

(To face

3rd General Direction, Artillery Material.

4th General Direction, Engineer Material.

5th General Direction, Military Maps.

8th G Dire Admin and S

1st Bureau, Technical Matters (2 sections).

2nd Bureau, Accounts.

1st Bureau, Technical Matters (2 sections).

2nd Bureau, Accounts (2 sections).

1st Bureau, General Duties.

2nd Bureau, Special Duties.

Cab Director

1st Direction, Administration.

2nd Direction, Supply.

1st Bur Funds Lodging and Travelling Allowances (2 sections).

nd Bureau, Audit.

3rd Bureau, General Accounts.

4th Bureau, Civil Personnel.

5th Bureau, War Office Material.

6th Bureau, Clothing and Equipment.

7th Bureau, Remount, Bedding, and Camp Equipment.

8th Bureau, Rations and Transport.

9t P

Th

The Mi

Minist

Secretariat and

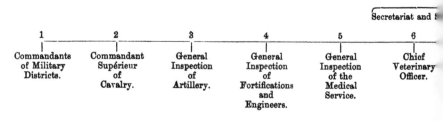

1	2	3	4	5	6
Commandants of Military Districts.	Commandant Supérieur of Cavalry.	General Inspection of Artillery.	General Inspection of Fortifications and Engineers.	General Inspection of the Medical Service.	Chief Veterinary Officer.

(8674)

(*To face p.* 124.)

LE II.

THE HIGH COMMANDS AND SERVICES OF THE ARMY.

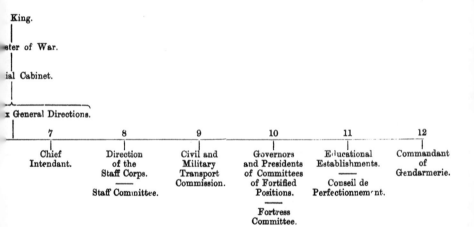

King.

ster of War.

ial Cabinet.

x General Directions.

7	8	9	10	11	12
Chief Intendant.	Direction of the Staff Corps. ——— Staff Committee.	Civil and Military Transport Commission.	Governors and Presidents of Committees of Fortified Positions. ——— Fortress Committee.	Educational Establishments. ——— Conseil de Perfectionnement.	Commandant of Gendarmerie.

TABLE III.

MILITARY PERSONNEL AT THE WAR OFFICE.

Ranks.	Arms.							Total.
	General Staff.	Staff Corps.	Intendance.	Infantry.	Cavalry.	Artillery.	Engineers.	
Officers—								
Major-General ...	1	—	1	—	—	—	—	2
Colonel ...	—	1	1	—	—	—	1	3
Lieut.-Colonel ...	—	2	—	1	—	—	1	4
Major ...	—	2	—	—	—	1	—	3
Captain Commandant	—	5	5	7	1	2	1	21
Captain ...	—	—	—	8	—	3	2	13
Lieutenant ...	—	—	1	30	—	3	—	34
								80
N.C.O.'s and Men—								
Sous-Officers ...	—	—	—	—	—	—	—	70
Corporals ...	—	—	—	—	—	—	—	6
Privates ...	—	—	—	—	—	—	—	51
								127
Total ...	1	10	8	46	1	9	5	207

FIELD NOTES ON THE BELGIAN, FRENCH AND GERMAN ARMIES.

PART I.—BELGIUM.

CHAPTER I.

WAR ORGANIZATION, NUMBERS AND ESTABLISHMENTS OF THE BELGIAN ARMY.

(*a.*) TOTAL NUMBERS AVAILABLE ON MOBILIZATION.

The Belgian Government has decided that a total force of 340,000 men is required for the defence of the country, and that they should be allotted as follows :—

> 150,000 men to the field army.
> 130,000 men to the garrisons of fortresses.
> 60,000 men to the reserve and auxiliary troops.

The number of men Belgium can mobilize depends in the first place upon whether or no her mobilization is interrupted. A hostile invasion during the process of mobilization would seriously derange the railway traffic throughout the country, and would probably prevent the reservists of some districts from rejoining the Colours. But, in any case, 340,000 men will not be available until 1926. If mobilization is uninterrupted, it is calculated that in 1914 Belgium could mobilize 210,000 men, and by 1917 255,000 men will be available. It is probable that from 100,000 to 130,000 of these would be allotted to the garrisons of the fortresses, and the remainder to the field army.

(*b.*) GENERAL ORGANIZATION OF THE ARMY.

Field Army.

The field army is organized in general headquarters (to which are attached certain army troops), 6 divisions, and a cavalry division. For details, *see* War Organization and Establishments, page 5, and Order of Battle, page 13.

Composition of a division.

Divisional headquarters.
3 mixed brigades (*a*).
1 divisional cavalry regiment.
1 divisional artillery regiment (*b*).
1 engineer battalion.
1 telegraph section.
1 transport corps.

Composition of the cavalry division.

Cavalry divisional headquarters.
3 cavalry brigades (*c*).
1 cyclist battalion.
1 horse artillery group.
1 cyclist pioneer-bridging company.
1 telegraph section.
1 transport corps.

Composition of a mixed brigade.

Mixed brigade headquarters.
2 infantry regiments (*d*).
1 artillery group.
1 platoon of gendarmerie.

Composition oj a cavalry brigade.

Cavalry brigade headquarters.
2 cavalry regiments.

(*a.*) The 3rd and 4th divisions each contain four mixed brigades, the additional mixed brigades being intended for the mobile defence of Liége and Namur respectively.

(*b.*) The divisional artillery regiments are each to consist of headquarters, 1 group of field batteries, and 2 groups of howitzer batteries, but at the beginning of 1914 the howitzer batteries have not yet been raised. The divisional artillery regiment of the 2nd division contains a second (extra) group of field batteries, and that of the 6th division contains an extra group of horse batteries.

(*c.*) In 1914 the 3rd cavalry brigade does not exist.

(*d.*) Only one of these regiments per brigade has a machine-gun company.

Fortress Troops.

(For details, *see* Order of Battle, page 13.)

Antwerp.—It is intended to form on mobilization a division of fortress troops for Antwerp. This division would have much the same composition as a division of the field army, but would be composed of units which exist in peace as weak cadres only, and would be filled up with the older classes of reservists on mobilization.

In addition to this division, there are also garrison, coast, and siege artillery units to man the guns of the fortress, and the infantry defence of the works is to be undertaken by second reserve and depôt batteries formed of spare artillery reservists, and by dismounted squadrons formed of spare cavalry reservists. There are also engineer and transport units, and administrative services and departments.

Liége and Namur.—The 14th and 13th mixed brigades are respectively detailed for the mobile defence of these fortresses, but it is intended to replace them as soon as possible after mobilization by fortress mixed brigades, to be formed in a similar manner to the fortress division for Antwerp. There are also fortress artillery and engineer units, and administrative services and departments.

(c.) WAR ORGANIZATION AND ESTABLISHMENTS.

N.B.—In the event of mobilization during 1914, or for 3 or 4 years afterwards, the strength of mobilized units would in most cases be below their full war establishment.

Field Army.

N.B.—When the figures under "Vehicles" are shown as a fraction, the numerator represents horse-drawn vehicles, the denominator represents motors : thus 4/1 represents 4 horse-drawn vehicles and 1 motor.

Unit.	Total number of				
	Officers and men.	Horses.	Guns.	Machine guns.	Vehicles.
Infantry.					
1 company (*a*) (*d*)	264	...	...	...	...
1 battalion (headquarters and 4 companies) (*b*) (*d*).	1,067	2	...	...	...
1 machine gun company	71	...	...	6	12
1 regiment (headquarters, 3 battalions and 1 machine-gun company) (*c*) (*d*).	3,324	10	...	6	12
1 regiment (headquarters and 3 battalions) (*c*) (*d*).	3,214	10	...	...	...
2 regiments (infantry of a mixed brigade) (*d*).	6,538	20	...	6	12
Cyclists.					
1 company	156	...	...	...	...
1 battalion (headquarters and 3 companies)	477	2	...	...	...
Cavalry.					
1 squadron (divisional cavalry) (*e*)	138	139	...	...	...
1 squadron (cavalry division) (*e*)...	154	155	...	...	...
1 regiment (divisional cavalry: headquarters, 2 wing headquarters and 4 squadrons) (*f*).	587	593	...	...	...
1 regiment (cavalry division: headquarters, 2 wing headquarters and 4 squadrons) (*f*).	651	657	...	...	...
Artillery.					
1 field or howitzer battery (4 guns) (*g*) (*h*).	158	140	4	...	12
1 horse battery (4 guns) (*g*) ...	124	156	4	...	9
1 group field or howitzer batteries (mixed brigade or divisional artillery regiment: headquarters and 3 batteries) (*l*) (*h*).	493	442	12	...	37
1 group horse artillery (headquarters and 3 batteries) (*l*).	391	490	12	...	28
1 divisional artillery regiment (headquarters, 1 group field batteries) (*h*).	509	456	12	...	37

For notes, *see* page 12.

Unit.	Total number of				
	Officers and men.	Horses.	Guns.	Machine guns.	Vehicles.
Engineers.					
General headquarter telegraph platoon.	100	23	...	...	5/2
General headquarter aviation company.	175	...	...	...	(*k*)
General headquarter balloon company.	263	...	...	...	(*k*)
Divisional telegraph section ...	59	19	...	...	4/1
Pioneer-bridging company (*m*) ...	253	25	...	...	6
Pioneer company (*m*)	225	25	...	...	6
Divisional engineer battalion (*b*) (headquarters, 1 pioneer-bridging company and 1 pioneer company).	486	52	...	...	12
Cyclist pioneer-bridging company (*m*) (cavalry division).	215	27	...	...	4
Cyclist telegraph section (cavalry division).	28	...	...	...	/1
Divisional Transport Corps.					
1st company—infantry ammunition columns (*o*).	366	359	...	...	87/20
2nd company—artillery ammunition columns (*n*) (*o*).	387	348	...	...	50/45
3rd company—ambulance, engineer park camping gear (*o*).	630	349	...	...	66/
4th company—butchery and supplies (*p*).	371	200	...	...	41/56
5th company—baggage (*q*)... ...	146	190	...	...	59/
6th company—ambulance, P.O., reserve motors, and supplies (*r*).	450	76	...	...	16/116
Divisional transport corps headquarters.	7	6	...	...	...
Total divisional transport corps (1st, 2nd and 5th divisions).	2,357	1,528	...	...	319/237
Total divisional transport corps (3rd division) (*s*).	2,594	1,772	...	...	376/237

For notes, *see* page 12.

Unit.	Total number of				
	Officers and men.	Horses.	Guns.	Machine guns.	Vehicles.
Total divisional transport corps (4th division) (*s*).	2,592	1,768	...	...	374/237
Total divisional transport corps (6th division) (*t*).	2,360	1,534	...	...	322/237
Ambulance column (cavalry division) (*o*).	148	60	...	...	15/
Engineer park (cavalry division) (*o*).	79	108	...	...	16/
Motor ammunition column (cavalry division) (*o*).	46	...	...	...	/15
Motor butchery (cavalry division) (*p*).	38	...	...	...	/10
Motor supply column (cavalry division) (*p*).	81	...	...	...	/25
Baggage train and *service de l'arrière* (cavalry division).	341	...	...	...	/47
Headquarters cavalry divisional transport corps.	9	9	...	...	...
Total cavalry divisional transport corps.	742	177	...	...	31/97
Larger units.—Mixed brigade.					
Headquarters...	15	8	...	...	...
Infantry: 2 regiments and 1 ma-chine-gun company.	6,538	20	...	6	12
Artillery: 1 group	493	442	12	...	37
Gendarmerie: 1 platoon	32	32	...	...	...
Total, mixed brigade	7,078	513	12	6	49
Total, 13th mixed brigade (dif-ferent establishment for in-fantry) (*d*).	5,494	502	12	6	49
Total, 14th mixed brigade (dif-ferent establishment for in-fantry) (*d*).	7,100	506	12	6	49

For notes, *see* page 12.

Unit.	Total number of				
	Officers and men.	Horses.	Guns.	Machine guns.	Vehicles.
Cavalry brigade.					
Headquarters...	14	11	...	...	...
2 regiments	1,032	1,314	...	...	...
Total cavalry brigade	1,316	1,325	...	...	...
Division.					
Headquarters...	93	68	...	...	1/3
3 mixed brigades ... ... ● ...	21,234	1,506	36	18	147
Divisional cavalry regiment ...	587	593	...	...	...
Divisional artillery regiment (*h*) ...	509	456	12	...	37
Divisional engineers	545	71	...	...	16/1
Transport corps (*n*)	2,357	1,528	...	...	319/237
Total, 1st or 5th divisons (*h*) (*n*)	25,325	4,222	48	18	420/241
Total, 2nd division (*h*) (*n*) (*v*) ...	25,818	4,664	60	18	457/241
Total, 3rd division (*d*) (*h*) (*n*) (*x*)	32,662	4,972	60	18	626/241
Total, 4th division (*d*) (*h*) (*n*) (*x*)	31,054	4,964	60	18	624/241
Total, 6th division (*h*) (*n*) (*t*) ...	25,726	4,718	60	18	563/241
Cavalry division.					
Headquarters...	58	59	...	...	/3
2 cavalry brigades (*u*)	2,632	2,650	...	...	...
Cyclist battalion	477	2	...	...	...
Horse artillery group	391	490	12	...	28
Cavalry divisional engineers ...	242	27	...	...	4/1
Cavalry divisional transport corps	742	177	...	...	31/97
Total cavalry division	4,538	3,405	12	...	63/101
General headquarters	198	136	...	...	9/5
Army troops.					
Telegraph platoon	100	23	...	...	7
Aviation company	175	...	...	...	(*k*)
Balloon company	263	...	...	...	(*k*)
Gendarmerie detachment	103	46	...	...	...
Total general headquarters and army troops.	839	205	...	...	(*k*)

For notes *see* page 12.

(*a*) The company has 3 platoons, the platoon 2 sections, and the section 2 squads. A captain commands the company, a subaltern or warrant officer the platoon, a serjeant the section, and a corporal the squad. If mobilized during 1914, companies will only have 2 platoons instead of 3, owing to shortage of men.

(*b*) A major commands the battalion.

(*c*) The regiment with the lowest number in each mixed brigade is the active regiment, is commanded by a colonel, and has a machine-gun company; the other regiment is the *régiment bis* is commanded by a lieutenant-colonel, and has no machine-gun company.

(*d*) The 13th and 14th regiments of the line, and the 33rd and 34th (their *régiments bis*) are intended for the mobile defence of Namur and Liége, respectively, and have a special organization : each company has a supplementary platoon, which forms the garrison of a fort; the battalions each consist of headquarters and 3 companies; and the 14th and 34th regiments each contain 4 battalions.

(*e*) The squadron has 4 platoons, the platoon 2 sections, and the section 2 squads ; the ranks of their commanders are the same as those in an infantary company, but the equivalent of an infantry serjeant is a *maréchal des logis* in the cavalry.

(*f*) The regiment is commanded by a colonel or lieutenant-colonel; the group (2 or 3 squadrons) by a major.

(*g*) A battery is commanded by a captain, and has 2 sections, each commanded by a subaltern.

(*h*) No howitzer batteries have been formed at the beginning of 1914, but it is intended to raise 2 groups each of 3 howitzer batteries for the divisional artillery regiment of each division, which will then consist of headquarters, 1 group field batteries, and 2 groups howitzer batteries.

(*k*) Number varies.

(*l*) A group is commanded by a lieutenant-colonel or major.

(*m*) A company is commanded by a captain, and has 3 platoons, each commanded by a subaltern or warrant officer.

(*n*) Does not include the howitzer ammunition columns, which have not yet been formed (1914).

(*o*) These form the *train de combat*.

(*p*) *Train de vivres.*

(*q*) *Train de bagages.*

(*r*) *Service divisionnaire de l'arrière.*

(*s*) Stronger to allow for the additional mixed brigade in each of these divisions.

(*t*) The 6th division contains an (extra) group of horse artillery.

(*u*) It is intended to form a 3rd cavalry brigade, but this has not yet been done (1914).

(*v*) The 2nd division has a second (extra) group of field batteries in its divisional artillery regiment ; this extra group is eventually to be converted into one of the groups of howitzer batteries, when they are formed.

(*x*) The 3rd and 4th divisions each contain a fourth (extra) mixed brigade, intended for the mobile defence of Liége and Namur, respectively.

(*d.*) ORDER OF BATTLE.

Field Army.

General Headquarters—
Telegraph platoon.
Aviation company.
Balloon company.
Gendarmerie detachment.

1st Division—
1st divisional headquarters.
2nd mixed brigade—
2nd mixed brigade headquarters.
2nd line regiment.
22nd line regiment.
2nd mixed brigade artillery group—1st, 2nd and
3rd batteries.
Platoon of gendarmerie.

3rd mixed brigade—
3rd mixed brigade headquarters.
3rd line regiment.
23rd line regiment.
3rd mixed brigade artillery group—4th, 5th and
6th batteries.
Platoon of gendarmerie.

4th mixed brigade—
4th mixed brigade headquarters.
4th line regiment.
24th line regiment.
4th mixed brigade artillery group—7th, 8th and
9th batteries.
Platoon of gendarmerie.
3rd lancers.
1st artillery regiment—10th, 11th and 12th batteries.
1st divisional engineer battalion.
1st divisional transport corps.
Telegraph section.

2nd Division—

2nd divisional headquarters.
5th mixed brigade —
    5th mixed brigade headquarters.
    5th line regiment.
    25th line regiment.
    5th mixed brigade artillery group—19th, 20th and
        21st batteries.
    Platoon of gendarmerie.

6th mixed brigade—
    6th mixed brigade headquarters.
    6th line regiment.
    26th line regiment.
    6th mixed brigade artillery group—22nd, 23rd and
        24th batteries.
    Platoon of gendarmerie.

7th mixed brigade—
    7th mixed brigade headquarters.
    7th line regiment.
    27th line regiment.
    7th mixed brigade artillery group—25th, 26th and
        27th batteries.
    Platoon of gendarmerie.

4th *chasseurs à cheval* (provisionally).
2nd artillery regiment—
    I. group—28th, 29th and 30th batteries.
    II. group—31st, 32nd and 33rd batteries.

2nd divisional engineer battalion.
2nd divisional transport corps.
    Telegraph section.

3rd Division.

3rd divisional headquarters.
9th mixed brigade—
    9th mixed brigade headquarters.
    9th line regiment.
    29th line regiment.
    9th mixed brigade artillery group—43rd, 44th and
        45th batteries.
    Platoon of gendarmerie.

3rd Division—*continued.*

11th mixed brigade—

11th mixed brigade headquarters.
11th line regiment.
31st line regiment.
11th mixed brigade artillery group—37th, 38th and 39th batteries.
Platoon of gendarmerie.

12th mixed brigade—

12th mixed brigade headquarters.
12th line regiment.
32nd line regiment.
12th mixed brigade artillery group—40th, 41st and 42nd batteries.
Platoon of gendarmerie.

14th mixed brigade—

14th mixed brigade headquarters.
14th line regiment.
34th line regiment.
14th mixed brigade artillery group—46th, 47th and 48th batteries.
Platoon of gendarmerie.

2nd lancers.

3rd artillery regiment—49th, 50th and 51st batteries.

3rd divisional engineer battalion.

3rd divisional transport corps.
Telegraph section.

4th Division.

4th divisional headquarters.

8th mixed brigade—

8th mixed brigade headquarters.
8th line regiment.
28th line regiment.
8th mixed brigade artillery group—58th, 59th and 60th batteries.
Platoon of gendarmerie.

4th Division—*continued.*

    10th mixed brigade—

        10th mixed brigade headquarters.
        10th line regiment.
        30th line regiment.
        10th mixed brigade artillery group—64th, 65th and 66th batteries.
        Platoon of gendarmerie.

    13th mixed brigade—

        13th mixed brigade headquarters.
        13th line regiment.
        33rd line regiment.
        13th mixed brigade artillery group—67th, 68th and 69th batteries.
        Platoon of gendarmerie.

    15th mixed brigade—

        15th mixed brigade headquarters.
        1st rifles.
        4th rifles.
        15th mixed brigade artillery group—61st, 62nd and 63rd batteries.
        Platoon of gendarmerie.

    1st lancers.
    4th artillery regiment—70th, 71st and 72nd batteries.
    4th divisional engineer battalion.
    4th divisional transport corps.
        Telegraph section.

5th Division.

    5th divisional headquarters.
    1st mixed brigade—

        1st mixed brigade headquarters.
        1st line regiment.
        21st line regiment.
        1st mixed brigade artillery group—79th, 80th and 81st batteries.
        Platoon of gendarmerie.

5th Division—*continued.*
  16th mixed brigade—
    16th mixed brigade headquarters.
    2nd rifles.
    5th rifles.
    16th mixed brigade artillery group—82nd, 83rd and
      84th batteries.
    Platoon of gendarmerie.

  17th mixed brigade—
    17 mixed brigade headquarters.
    3rd rifles.
    6th rifles.
    17th mixed brigade artillery group—85th, 86th and
      87th batteries.
    Platoon of gendarmerie.
  2nd *chasseurs à cheval.*
  5th artillery regiment—88th, 89th and 90th batteries.
  5th divisional engineer battalion.
  5th divisional transport corps.
    Telegraph section.

6th Division.

  6th divisional headquarters.

  18th mixed brigade—
    18th mixed brigade headquarters.
    1st grenadiers.
    2nd grenadiers.
    18th mixed brigade artillery group—97th, 98th and
      99th batteries.
    Platoon of gendarmerie.

  19th mixed brigade—
    19th mixed brigade headquarters.
    1st carabiniers.
    3rd carabiniers.
    19th mixed brigade artillery group—100th, 101st
      and 102nd batteries.
    Platoon of gendarmerie.

B

6th Division—*continued.*
20th mixed brigade—
20th mixed brigade headquarters.
2nd carabiniers.
4th carabiniers.
20th mixed brigade artillery group—103rd, 104th
and 105th batteries.
Platoon of gendarmerie.

1st *chasseurs à cheval.*

6th artillery regiment—
I. group—106th, 107th and 108th batteries.
IV. group—4th, 5th and 6th horse batteries.
6th divisional engineer battalion.
6th divisional transport corps.
Telegraph section.

Cavalry division—

Cavalry divisional headquarters.

1st cavalry brigade—
1st cavalry brigade headquarters.
1st guides.
2nd guides.

2nd cavalry brigade—
2nd cavalry brigade headquarters.
4th lancers.
5th lancers.

3rd cavalry brigade (not yet formed, 1914).
Cyclist battalion.
Cavalry divisional horse artillery group—1st, 2nd and
3rd horse batteries.
Cyclist pioneer-bridging company.
Cavalry divisional transport corps.
Telegraph section.

Fortress Troops.
Antwerp garrison—

Fortress headquarters.
Headquarters for each section of the defence—6 sections
in first line, 2 sections in second line, 1 section
Antwerp City.

Regiment of garrison artillery—headquarters, 1st to 20th active batteries, 21st to 25th first reserve batteries (cadres in peace), 20 second reserve and 5 depôt batteries (non-existent in peace).

Regiment of coast artillery—headquarters, 1st to 3rd active batteries, 4th to 6th first reserve batteries (cadres in peace), 3 second reserve and 1 depôt battery (non-existent in peace).

Regiment of siege artillery—headquarters, 1st to 16th active batteries, 17th to 20th reserve batteries and siege park (cadres in peace), 4 depôt batteries (non-existent in peace).

Regiment of fortress engineers—headquarters, 1st and 2nd active battalions, and 3rd to 6th reserve battalions (cadres in peace).

Railway company of engineers.

Telegraph company of engineers.

Aviation company of engineers.

Torpedo company of engineers.

Balloon company of engineers.

Service of fortification.

Transport corps.

Territorial establishments : intendance, medical and administrative.

Fortress infantry regiments : number uncertain, probably 12, the 1st to 7th line, the 2nd and 3rd rifles, the 1st and 2nd carabiniers, and the grenadiers.

Fortress cavalry squadrons : probably 4.

Fortress field artillery batteries : 1st to 18th reserve field batteries, to be formed by 8 reserve field batteries of the 1st, 2nd, 5th and 6th divisions.

It is intended to form on mobilization a fortress division for Antwerp : this division would presumably be more or less mobile, and would be additional to the actual garrisons of the works. It could probably be formed as follows :—

Antwerp Fortress Division—

Divisional headquarters : non-existent in peace improvised.

(3505) **B 2**

3 mixed brigades :—each—

> Headquarters : improvised ; non-existant in peace.
> 2 to 4 fortress infantry regiments.
> 1 group fortress field artillery : 1st to 9th reserve field batteries, 3 to each group, very weak cadres in peace.
> 1 platoon of gendarmerie (or civic guard).

Fortress cavalry regiment : headquarters and 2 wing headquarters improvised, non-existent in peace ; 4 squadrons.

Fortress divisional artillery regiment : headquarters and 3 groups each of 3 batteries, 10th to 18th reserve field batteries, very weak cadres in peace.

Fortress divisional engineer battalion and telegraph section : to be improvised from the regiment of fortress engineers.

Fortress divisional transport corps.

It is intended that the 20 second reserve and 5 depôt batteries of garrison artillery should undertake the infantry defence of the works occupied by the active and first reserve batteries of the regiment : the 3 second reserve and 1 depôt battery of coast artillery undertake the same duty for the active and first reserve batteries of their regiment : and the 4 depôt batteries of siege artillery undertake the same duty for the reserve batteries of their regiment.

The total strength of the garrison required for Antwerp has been fixed at 90,000 men.

Liége Garrison—

> Fortress headquarters.
> 4 battalions of fortress artillery, one for each sector of the defences (4 battalion headquarters, 1st to 12th active batteries, and 13th to 16th reserve batteries).
> 1 battalion of fortress engineers (headquarters and 3 active companies).
> 1 depôt of technical troops.
> 1 transport corps.
> Territorial establishments : intendance, medical and administrative.

Fortress infantry regiments : probably 9th, 11th, 12th and 14th.

Fortress field artillery batteries : 1 group, 19th to 21st reserve field batteries, formed by the two reserve batteries of the 3rd division.

The 14th mixed brigade of the 3rd division is detailed for the mobile defence of Liége : but it is intended that it should be relieved as soon as possible by a fortress mixed brigade, composed as follows :—

Liége fortress mixed brigade—

Headquarters : improvised, non-existent in peace.
2 to 4 fortress infantry regiments.
1 group of fortress field artillery.
1 platoon of gendarmerie (or civic guard).

The strength of the garrison required by Liége has been fixed at 23,000 men.

Namur garrison—

Fortress headquarters.
3 battalions of fortress artillery, 1 for each sector of the defence : 3 battalion headquarters, 1st to 9th active batteries, 10th to 12th reserve batteries.
1 battalion of fortress engineers : headquarters and 3 active companies.
1 depôt of technical troops.
1 transport corps.
Territorial establishments : intendance, medical and administrative.
Fortress infantry regiments : probably 8th, 10th, 13th and 1st rifles.
Fortress field artillery batteries : 1 group, 32nd to 24th reserve field batteries, formed by the 2 reserve batteries of the 4th division.

The 13th mixed brigade of the 4th division is detailed for the mobile defence of Namur, but it is intended to relieve it as soon as possible by a fortress mixed brigade, to be formed as at Liége.

The strength of the garrison required for Namur has been fixed at 18,000 men.

CHAPTER II.

UNIFORMS OF BELGIAN TROOPS. MILITARY HIERARCHY AND BADGES OF RANK. ARMAMENT, AND AMMUNITION AND TOOLS CARRIED IN THE FIELD.

(*a.*) FIELD SERVICE UNIFORM.

Corps.	Jacket (field service).	Trousers or overalls.	Head-dress.	Cloak or greatcoat.
General officers ...	Dark blue, cherry-coloured braid.	Dark blue	... ...	Dark blue.
Staff officers ...	Dark green, cherry-coloured braid.	Dark green, cherry-coloured stripes.	Dark green shako	Dark green.
Infantry— Infantry of the Line.	Dark blue	Blue - grey, scarlet piping.	Blue shako, trimmed red.	Dark blue.
Officers ...	Dark blue, grey facings.	Blue-grey, dark blue stripes.	,, ,,	,,
Chasseurs à pied ...	Dark green, yellow facings.	Blue - grey, yellow piping.	Dark green shako	Dark green.
Officers ...	,, ,,	Blue-grey, dark green stripes.	,,	,,

Grenadiers ...	Dark blue, scarlet facings.	Dark blue, broad red stripes.	Bearskin cap ...	Dark blue, red facings, regimental badge on collar.
Officers ...	" "	Black, scarlet stripes...	"	" "
Carabiniers,...	As for *Chasseurs à pied*	As for *Chasseurs à pied* ...	Special felt hat ...	As for *Chasseurs à pied.*
Cavalry— *Chasseurs à cheval*	Dark blue; facings, 1st regt. yellow, 2nd regt. red.	Blue - grey, white stripes.	Blue shako ...	Dark blue, with cape.
Officers ...	Dark blue, scarlet facings.	Dark blue stripes ...	"	" "
Guides ...	Green, cherry-coloured piping. Number of regiment on collar.	Cherry-coloured, yellow stripes.	Black busby, cherry-coloured bag.	Green.
Officers ...	" "	Cherry-coloured, green stripes.	" "	"
Lancers ...	Dark blue; facings, 1st regt. cherry-coloured, 2nd regt. yellow, 3rd regt. white, 4th regt. blue.	Blue - grey; 1st and 2nd, white stripes; 3rd and 4th, yellow stripes.	Lance cap ...	As for *Chasseurs.*
Officers ...	Dark blue; facings, 1st, 2nd and 3rd regts. cherry-coloured, 4th and 5th regts. scarlet.	Blue-grey, dark blue stripes.	"	"

Corps.	Jacket (field service).	Trousers or overalls.	Head-dress.	Cloak or greatcoat.
Artillery ...	As for infantry, with number of regiment or initial of fortress group on shoulder strap.	Dark grey, broad red stripes.	Field and horse, busby; fortress, shako.	Dark blue, field and horse, cavalry pattern; fortress, infantry pattern, with red facings.
Officers ...	Dark blue, scarlet facings.	Black, scarlet stripes	Gold lines ...	,, ,,
Engineers ...	As for infantry, red facings.	Dark blue, broad red stripes.	Shako, red ball ...	As for infantry, with red facings and regimental badge.
Officers	Dark blue, scarlet and black facings.	,, ,,	,, ,, ,,	,, ,,
Medical ...	Dark blue, cherry-coloured facings.	Black, cherry-coloured stripes.	Cocked hat ...	As for infantry.
Transport corps ...	Dark blue, sky-blue piping. •	Dark blue ...	Shako, green ball	Dark blue, light blue facings.
Officers ...	,, ,,	Black, light blue stripes.	,, ,,	,, ,,
Administrative battalion.	Dark blue, light-blue piping.	Dark blue ...	Blue shako, light blue ball.	Dark blue.
Officers ...	,, ,,	Dark blue, light blue stripes.	Cocked hat ...	Dark blue, light blue facings.
Cyclists ...	Dark green, yellow facings.	Blue grey, yellow piping.	Round cap with peak in front, yellow band	Dark green.
Officers ...	As for carabiniers ...	As for carabiniers ...	Képi ...	,, ,,

Gendarmerie ...	Dark blue, white and scarlet aiguillettes shoulder straps (mounted men). Dark blue, red facings, white auguillettes (dismounted men).	Dark blue breeches (mounted men). Dark blue trousers, red stripe (dismounted men).	Bearskin cap or képi.	Dark blue.
Officers ...	Dark blue, scarlet facings.	Oxford grey ...	,,	Dark blue, scarlet facings.

N.B.—In service dress infantry, fortress artillery, engineers, dismounted men of field artillery and administrative battalion wear the greatcoat. Officers of all arms, cyclists and mounted men do not usually wear it.

(b.) RANKS

Belgian rank.	English equivalent.
Corporal (infantry) ... ... Brigadier (mounted troops)	} Corporal.
Sergent (infantry) ... ... *Maréchal-des-logis* (mounted troops)	} Serjeant.
Sergent fourrier	Company quartermaster-serjeant.
Maréchal-des-logis-fourrier ...	Squadron quartermaster-serjeant.
Sergent-major	Company serjeant-major.
Maréchal-des-logis-chef ...	Squadron serjeant-major.
Premier sergent	Battalion serjeant-major.
Premier maréchal - des - logis- chef.	Regimental serjeant-major.
Adjutant-sous-officier ...	1st class warrant officer.
Sous-lieutenant	Second lieutenant.
Lieutenant	Lieutenant.
Capitaine en second	Captain, 2nd in command of company or squadron.
Capitaine commandant ...	Major or captain commanding a squadron or company.
Major (commands a battalion)	Major.
Lieutenant-colonel	Lieutenant-colonel.
Colonel	Colonel.
Général-major	Major-general.
Lieutenant-général	Lieutenant-general.

(c.) ARMAMENT.

Infantry and engineers—

Mauser rifle, 1889 pattern, ·301-inch calibre, magazine holds 5 cartridges ; muzzle velocity, 1,968 feet per second ; weight of rifle, 8 lb. 10 oz.

Sword bayonet ; length of rifle with bayonet, 5 feet ; weight of bayonet, 1 lb.

Officers : sword and Browning pistol, ·301 inch calibre.

Cavalry—

    Sword, lance, carbine. (It is intended to arm all cavalry with the lance, but in 1914 *chasseurs à cheval* have not yet received it.)

    The present bamboo lances are to be replaced by hollow steel lances.

    Mauser carbine, 1889 pattern, ·301 inch calibre, magazine holds 5 cartridges; muzzle velocity, 1,709 feet per second; weight of carbine, 6 lb. 2 oz.

Horse and field artillery— .

    Krupp 2·95-inch (7·5 cm.) Q.F. gun ; range, 6,000 metres (claimed); rate of fire 10 to 15 rounds a minute. Fires shrapnel and high explosive shell. Proportion of high explosive shell to shrapnel carried in the field as 1 to 8 or 10.

(d.) SUPPLY OF AMMUNITION.

Approximate number of rounds per gun or rifle carried in the field.

Arm.	On the man.	On the gun and limber.	On the battery wagons.	1st infantry ammunition column.	2nd infantry ammunition column.	3rd infantry ammunition column.	4th infantry ammunition column.	Motor infantry ammunition column.	1st artillery ammunition column.	2nd artillery ammunition column.	3rd artillery ammunition column.	1st artillery motor ammunition column.	2nd artillery motor ammunition column.	3rd artillery motor ammunition column.	Total.
Infantry...	120	...	...	25	25	25	25	25	...	...	...	...	...	...	245
Machine guns ...	...	500	3 500	11,000	...	...	...	...	...	...	...	...	...	...	15,000
Field artillery— 1st, 2nd, 5th and 6th divisions.	...	32	303	...	...	...	...	...	50	50	...	42	42	42	561
3rd and 4th divisions	...	32	303	...	...	...	...	...	33	33	33	40	40	40	554
Horse artillery— Cavalry division ...	...	32	186	...	...	...	...	...	...	...	...	150	...	...	368

(e.) Tools carried in the Field.

Unit.	On the person.						
	Entrenching implement.	Bill-hooks.	Hand axes.	Saws.	Wire-cutters.	Files.	Pincers.
Infantry company, field army ...	234	12	6	6	12	1	1
Infantry company, fortress regiment	84	12	3	6	9	1	1
Cyclist company	30	12	3	6	16	1	1

The short-handled Linneman entrenching implement at present in use is to be gradually replaced in the field army by the Brouyère–Spaak telescopic shovel.

CHAPTER III

MARCHES, OUTPOSTS, BILLETS.

(a.) MARCHES.

Infantry.—Pace 29½ inches, 120 to the minute. About 2½ miles an hour, including halts. An average day's march is reckoned at about 14 miles.

Cavalry.—Walk 110 to 120 yards a minute. Trot 220 to 280 yards a minute. Trot and walk 5 to 6½ miles an hour.

Artillery.—About the same paces as cavalry.

Distances on the march in rear of a—

Company	11 yards.
Squadron, battery, or equivalent unit ...	22 ,,
Battalion, group, or equivalent unit ...	33 ,,
Regiment	44 ,,
Brigade	66 ,,

Halts.—Ten minutes in each hour, or sometimes in easy country every two hours.

Advanced and rear-guards and order of march.—Much the same as in the British Army.

(b.) OUTPOSTS.

The Belgian formations correspond roughly to British formations as follows :—

(1.) *Postes d'avis*...	Advanced posts.
(2.) *Petit postes avec leurs senti- nelles.*	Picquets and sentries.
(3.) *Grand' gardes*	Supports.
(4.) *Soutien d'avant postes* ...	Reserves.

But in some respects (1) and (2) correspond more nearly to our picquets and supports respectively. *Grand' gardes* usually consist of a company, and furnish one or more *petits postes.* A *petit poste* may consist of a platoon, a section, or a squad, and is usually 400 to 600 yards from its *grand' garde*. Sentries are usually double. Sentries are relieved every hour or every two hours, and the two men forming a double sentry are never relieved together. *Postes d'avis* are usually furnished by the cavalry.

(c.) BILLETS.

Every house in a commune is numbered, and a list should be kept by the *secrétaire communal* (parish clerk), on which is shown the number of soldiers who may be billeted in each house in the commune in peace. When billeting in peace the Belgian military authorities always work in conjunction with the *bourgmestre* and *secrétaire communal* (mayor and parish clerk), and make their arrangements on the basis of this billeting census. In some communes the chief village which gives its name to the commune is smaller than some of the other villages in the commune ; these latter villages are known as *hameaux* (hamlets). As many communes are 2 to 3 miles in length, and some are as much as 8 miles long, and the billeting accommodation of a commune is afforded partly by the chief place, partly by its hamlets, it may often be important to find out quickly the distribution of houses in the commune. This can usually be discovered from the billeting census, if available, as it is arranged by hamlets. The boundaries of communes and the position of most of their hamlets are shown on the Belgian $\frac{1}{40000}$ map.

CHAPTER IV.

MISCELLANEOUS.

(*a.*) CLASSES OF PERSONS IN BELGIUM WHO MIGHT BE USEFUL AS GUIDES.

1. *Gardes champêtres* usually know their own communes well, and should be able to give detailed information as to roads, tracks and paths; they should also know about water, forage, horses, stock and vehicles.

2. *Gardes forestiers* know the woods in their own district well.

3. Rural postmen; many of them use bicycles, and cover long distances.

4. Cycle repairers; especially the official repairers to the Touring Club de Belgique; most of them are energetic cyclists, and know the roads well.

5. Drivers of tradesmen's carts; these supply most of the villages from the towns.

6. Country doctors and veterinary surgeons; their practice generally embraces a large area.

(*b.*) ABBREVIATIONS USED IN THE BELGIAN ARMY IN WRITING ORDERS.

Names of units are generally replaced by their initials; the numbers of regiments are written in large Arabic figures; those of battalions, squadrons, or artillery groups in Roman figures; those of companies, troops (*pelotons*) of cavalry and batteries in small Arabic figures as numerators.

Examples—

C.Q.G.	= *grand quartier général*	= general headquarters.
Q.G.	= *quartier général*	= headquarters (of an army or a division).

Examples—

D.A.	=*division d'armée*	=division.
D.C.	=*division de cavalerie*	=cavalry division.
Br. M.	=*brigade mixte*	=mixed brigade.
2	=*2e régiment de ligne*	=2nd regiment of the line.
E.M.	=*etat-major*	=headquarters of a brigade, regiment, wing, group ; or may mean the staff generally.

$\dfrac{\text{E.M. }^2/\text{III.}}{10}$ =Regimental headquarters and the 2nd company of the 3rd battalion of the 10th regiment of the line.

$\dfrac{\text{2 C. M.A.A.}}{\text{5 D.A.}}$ =The 2nd mechanical (automobile) artillery ammunition column of the 5th division.

$\dfrac{^{1\cdot 3}/\text{IV.}}{\text{2 G.}}$ =The 1st and 3rd troops (*pelotons*) of the 4th squadron of the 2nd regiment of guides.

2 Ch. ch. =2nd regiment of *chasseurs à cheval*.

C. = Carabiniers.

G. = Grenadiers (there is only one regiment of grenadiers).

Cy. = Cyclists.

+ = Ambulance.

$\dfrac{\text{E.M. II. III.}}{9}$ = Regimental headquarters and 2nd and 3rd battalions of the 9th regiment of the line.

P. = Field company (*pionniers*).

T. = Telegraphists.

$\dfrac{\text{1 cie.}/\text{I.}}{1}$ = A company of the 1st battalion of the 1st regiment of the line.

$\dfrac{\text{V.}}{\text{3 L.}}$ = The 5th squadron of the 3rd lancers.

$\dfrac{\text{E.M. 2 btns.}}{\text{2 Ch.}}$ = Regimental headquarters and two battalions of the 2nd *chasseurs à pied*.

(3505)   C

(c.) WALLOON AND FLEMING.

The Belgian nation, and Belgian regiments, are composed of two different races—the Walloons, who speak a sort of French, and the Flemings, who speak a sort of Dutch. Many Walloons can only talk French ; many Flemings can only talk Flemish. On the outbreak of a Franco-German war public opinion in Walloon districts is likely to be actively pro-French, whilst in Flemish districts, though hardly pro-French, is not likely to be actively pro-German. Both are Belgians first and foremost ; Walloons and Flemings only in second place. Belgian country people generally, and especially the Flemings, are very religious, and the large majority are Roman Catholics.